Author's Note

I have tried to recreate events, locales, and conversations from memory. In order to maintain anonymity for some individuals, I have, in some instances, changed or abbreviated their names and places. I may have changed some identifying characteristics and details, such as physical descriptions, occupations, and places of employment. Any resemblance between the resulting altered identities and actual persons, living or dead, is coincidental. If I have accidentally defamed, humiliated, or otherwise hurt someone's feelings as a result of them reading my memoir, be assured it is entirely unintentional. After all, I am the *Accidental P.I.*

PRAISE FOR *ACCIDENTAL P.I.*

"Fast paced, in-your-face, reads like a novel of police work in the turbulent sixties. The reader is back there looking over Dave's shoulder as it unfolds. The chapters on the Plainfield Riot and Officer John Gleason's murder are very moving. Having been 'on the job' myself, this book hits the mark."

Private Detective Dennis Harris,
TriCorps Security & Investigations
Retired Boston Homicide

"An accurate depiction of private investigations, if I ever saw one. We get a behind-the-scenes peek at real-life cases, often proving life is stranger than fiction. What more could one want: fraud, corporate corruption, murder, sex, tragic fatalities, and an exposé of the hypocrisy in our civil system . . . and all true!

Private Investigator Robert Higgins,
Skylands Detective Agency
Sergeant, New Jersey State Police, Retired

"Master investigator becomes master storyteller. Dave had me chuckling, nodding my head, and simply enjoying the ride. This is an honest, even if painful at times, look at real-life legal situations. And throughout, Dave and Linda's poignant journey is the thread that holds it all together. Way to go, Dave!"

Private Investigator Patrick Chase,
Florida Certified Investigator & Security Consultant
Captain, Minnesota State Police, Retired

"This book tells it like it really is—no holding back. My family has an eighty-year history in the private investigation field, and this book nails it. I know Dave and he has done it all, so the only thing left is to write about it. Dave, you son of a gun—you wrote my book. I love it."

Private Investigator Robert Simmons,
Simmons Agency, Inc.
Boston, Massachusetts

Accidental P.I.

ACCIDENTAL P.I.

A Private Investigator's
Fifty-Year Search
for the Facts

DAVID B. WATTS,
Private Investigator

DBWatts

MILL CITY PRESS

Mill City Press, Inc.
2301 Lucien Way #415
Maitland, FL 32751
407.339.4217
www.millcitypress.net

Cover Design by Alan Pranke

Typeset by MK Ross

Printed in the United States of America.

ISBN-13: 978-1-54566-411-7

In Memoriam

John Vincent Gleason, Jr.
1928–1967

~ Dedicated to my Linda Rose ~

She's my lively first mate and loving soul mate.
She follows my lead; yet her wisdom I heed.
Without her my travel would surely unravel.
Of this journey I plead, no more could one need.

Contents

PREFACE

A s a memoir should, this tells my story, but I hope you will see it as something more. My investigative career over the past fifty years and counting has spanned many cultural and social changes. As a young policeman, then detective, I experienced the turbulent sixties up close. The beginning of that decade saw law enforcement stagnated in a post-WWII mentality, but circumstances forced upgrades—so over the next several decades, the culture of the nightstick, whistle, brass call-box key, and six-shot revolver gave way to the Taser, pepper spray, portable radios, in-car video, computers, and European-style semi-automatic pistols. My journey witnessed all this and the underlying causes of these advancements.

My participation and experiences are told against the backdrop of this societal evolution. Lyndon Johnson's Civil Rights Act, the birth of political correctness, corporate greed, and the failings versus strengths of our legal system are all a part of my story. Perhaps better said: I was a part of those stories. I worked down in the trenches of investigation work. Whether in law enforcement or later on the civil side as a claims adjuster, then private investigator, my job was always to get the facts and let others sort them out. It was always in pursuit of the facts.

I claim no soapbox rights. I merely tell my story in the context of my surroundings and report my impressions of the times as I saw them. Bear in mind, of course, I was evolving, as well; while I can now look back through a more mature lens, my recollections and reactions are as firm now as they were when they happened. Time, the cumulative creature that it is, tends to bring events into better focus when hindsight is employed.

This is not an exposé or condemnation of any individual, group, or organization. Rather: the goal here is to pull back a few curtains and share the past five decades as I witnessed and lived them. Perhaps, it will provide a new perspective on law enforcement in general, real-life private investigation work vis-à-vis the movie version and some of the short comings of our legal system—though the latter is still better than any others.

What got me started on this memoir? A strong interest in history played a big role. My wife, Linda, and I are history buffs. We've visited every Civil War battlefield east of the Mississippi and more. Title searching brought us into contact with old deeds and mortgages. We also finished up our family trees after months of the usual genealogy research.

All this got me thinking about documenting my own experiences. More than just reminiscing, this writing experience was like hitting the pause button and second-guessing past events in my life. Admittedly, reliving some moments was uncomfortable, while others were satisfying. I recommend the exercise to anyone, but be prepared for an emotional experience. Most poignant were my memories of the Plainfield, New Jersey Riot and Officer John Gleason's murder investigation.

Again, this is not a tell-all tale. In some instances contractual restrictions apply. In others, there seemed no point in inflicting pain on anyone . . . even if some may deserve it. When appropriate, I opted not to identify individuals, especially those involved in lawsuits. In some cases, however, identity disclosure was necessary to tell the story adequately. These were purely subjective decisions. I am totally candid in my observations of individuals and events as I saw them at the time and since.

I undertook this project after reading a couple of books about writing one's memoir. Those how-to memoir books caution that the author should have something interesting to say and that there is in his or her past something worth writing about. My five-decade investigative career has been a fascinating journey that is, I believe, worth telling. I assume most of you have not sat on surveillance, gone on a drug raid, interviewed accused murderers, or testified in federal court. Perhaps the story of someone who has done all these things might grab your attention.

Mine has been a cumulative trek, as fate guided me into the private-investigation field—albeit through the hallways and byways of law enforcement and insurance claims.

Ergo my title: *Accidental P.I.* If it seems, as I brushed against those other fields while passing by, that my reportage is condescending, then I have missed the mark. In truth, I would not trade a moment of my "education" in any of those work venues. After all, the thirty-eight years I spent in private investigation is totally attributable to those earlier stops along the way.

Coming up with a title that nailed these past fifty years was tough. After all, part of the story is welcoming opportunities as they came along. Further, it would be disingenuous to claim this life of mine unfolded according to a master plan, because it just sort of happened accidently.

I tried out the proposed title on Linda, my wife of fifty-three years and my eternal sounding board. She thought for a moment, then offered a classic Linda response, "*Accidental P.U. . . . Reminiscences of an Old Poop* suits you better."

"Humor," we answer those who ask how to achieve marital longevity. Keep laughing and you don't have energy left to cry.

One would think working on real-life cases of horrible injury and death or going after the bad guys day after day would taint one's view of the human condition. Not so for us. Somehow, all that negativity makes us appreciate what we have and do our best to avoid discord and failure. I say "us" because Linda has been at my side throughout this journey, pitching in wherever possible. I know that without her my travel could not have gone as well as it did.

I stuck with my version of the title in spite of Linda's *On Golden Pond* suggestion. As you turn these pages, I hope you agree: while our journey has been somewhat accidental, we didn't exactly drift with the wind. If this book says anything, it is that the choices we make in life are important. But also don't forget this great quote from Woody Allen: "If you want to make God laugh, tell him your plans."

Dave B. Watts

ACCIDENTAL P.I.

Part One:

From Cop on the Beat to County Investigator

CHAPTER ONE

"Here He Comes!"

(Near the corner of West Fourth Street and Rushmore Avenue, just outside the city limits of Plainfield, New Jersey, early afternoon, spring 1965)

"What's the time now, David?"

"It's 1:35, Lieutenant." It would be a while before I'd be comfortable calling him Dan.

"He should be showing up any minute now."

"Who's that?"

Finally, I thought, *conversation. We've been parked in this car for a half hour not even making small talk, and I still don't know what this is about.*

"Howard Swint," Lieutenant Dan Hennessey answered without lowering the binoculars. "He's one of our numbers runners in town. You'll see a 1965 green Pontiac with NJ plate IDY-513 come in from Second Street any minute now. Wait, here he comes!"

The green Pontiac made a left and then a quick right into the driveway of 211 Rushmore Avenue. The dapper driver, a fortyish heavyset black man, sported a yellow golf shirt, green slacks, and pork pie hat. Scanning the entire neighborhood, he gingerly took the front steps, head swiveling back and forth. His gait—more like a strut—was slow and confident, his right wrist riding palm out just behind his right hip and left arm exaggerating its swing. He had that look of a little kid who just did something wrong and wondered if anyone was looking. Personal radar up and running, he jive-walked up the stairs and disappeared into the house.

Surely Hennessey had me here for a reason, so I played along. "How did you know he would show up here and now?"

"Surveillance, my boy, surveillance." Pink circular impressions remained around his eyes as a smiling Dan Hennessey handed over the binoculars. "We've been keeping tabs on this one. He's cagey, but I don't think he can spot us up here."

The lesson continued. "Swint is what we call a *known and convicted gambler*. Like most illegal gamblers, he pays more attention to his rearview mirror than the road ahead. As you saw, he walks around that way too." Still grinning, Hennessey added, "He gets busted again, and it's jail time." Our eyes stayed glued to Swint's Pontiac and the front porch of that house a quarter mile or so ahead. I still didn't have a clue as to why I was here with this somewhat mysterious detective lieutenant.

I was a twenty-five-year-old uniformed patrolman just back from a two-year stint in the U.S. Army and happy to get back "on the job," in cop-speak. Lieutenant Dan Hennessey's phone call that Saturday morning was, to say the least, unusual.

"Watts, Dan Hennessey here. Can you spare a couple of hours?" It was odd for a lieutenant detective to be calling on a lowly beat cop—especially a rookie like me. I shook off the cobwebs, just off my midnight shift.

"Sure, Lieutenant. What's up?"

Hennessey continued, "I'll pick you up at your apartment in an hour. I know you worked last night. Hope you don't mind."

I got dressed and was waiting at the curb when he pulled up in his own car.

"Ever Thought about Becoming a Cop?"

Let me catch you up. Before my two-year stint in the army, I had joined the boys in blue of the Plainfield, New Jersey, Police Department on March 21, 1961.

Some kids grow up and become just what they planned. They follow their dreams, get the required education, and go for it. Not me. I had no idea where I was going when I was twenty-one. They say that timing is everything in life, and I believe it. I was laid off from my job as a cost-accounting clerk with Lockheed Electronics on New Year's Eve, 1960. A few days later, I was walking around the block and ran into Patrolman Joseph Tufaro, a young giant of a fellow, casually walking his police beat. His chest stuck out and he stood ramrod straight. The nightstick danced in his hands. He was impressive.

"What are you doing hanging around?" he asked. "Shouldn't you be in school or working somewhere?" His attitude was friendly enough, but he had a good point. I explained that I was out looking for a job.

"Ever thought about becoming a cop? There are a few openings. Check it out."

It was just that simple. The events that followed included written, physical, and psychological exams, then being introduced to the mayor and council of the City of Plainfield one evening. It was there I first met my fellow recruits, David "Skippy" Saunderson and Bruce Tymeson, while waiting on the marble benches just outside the council chambers.

Bruce and I hit it off right away, and he was to become my best man when I married Linda, my high school sweetheart, a year later. A year after that, and to the day, I was Bruce's best man. First to wear these new khaki recruit uniforms, we were a novelty to the rest of the department, as well as the public. Topped off with dark blue U.S. Navy pea coats, we looked like a cross between over-aged boy scouts and half-out-of-uniform sailors.

Lieutenant George Campbell conducted our training at the police headquarters, as there wasn't much formal police training in those days. The old headquarters was a two-story block building constructed in the early 1900s at the corner of West Fourth Street and Cleveland Avenue in Plainfield. The façade was gray, foreboding, and it had green sconce-like lamps on either side of the entrance. One step up and inside the double doors brought you up against the chest-high sergeant's desk, New York City-style, just like those old black and white movies in the thirties and forties. The chief and patrol captain's offices were on either side of the entrance doors, and the municipal court was just off to the left. A corridor led to jail cells in the back. Upstairs were the identification and detective bureaus, along with the patrol shapeup room with its rows of lockers. It was truly a compact, old-fashioned police building when I started in 1961. It was also overcrowded and on its way out.

Lieutenant Campbell took his teaching position seriously. We buckled down, studying New Jersey state criminal statutes, police procedures, range qualifications . . . you name it. Later on, we did go for two weeks to a recruit class in Westfield with "newbies" from other departments, but the formal training ended there. We did not have several months of training at Sea Girt Police Academy, as they did decades later. The real schooling came from working on the job with experienced officers.

A City in Transition

In the early sixties, most of the fifty-five or so officers on the Plainfield department had served in World War II or Korea. They were a tough and confident bunch. The cop/doughnut relationship might have started right around then, because most were packing a few extra pounds. Our department was small enough to know everyone, yet was considered to be the one of the larger departments in central New Jersey. Only Elizabeth, the county seat of Union County, had a larger police department.

Plainfield in the fifties and sixties was a city in transition. Like most municipalities, it had its sections. The East Enders were mostly either children of Italian immigrants who arrived in the thirties or, as in the Sleepy Hollow section, wealthy stockbrokers and corporate executives in their expansive and expensive Tudor-style mansions. There was a small area in the East End where black people lived, mostly near the railroad tracks.

The city was bisected by the Central Jersey Railroad in an east/west direction, and for years those Sleepy Hollow executives in the East End would commute via rail to their offices in Newark and New York City.

The West End consisted of rows and rows of two-and-a-half-story frame houses in about an eighty-square-block area. This was a working-class neighborhood that originally housed factory workers for Mack Motors and other smaller companies located up and down the West Front Street and West Second Street areas. Most of Plainfield's black community lived in the West End.

The center of the city held the business district with several department stores and a smattering of small shops. Plainfield's businesses served folks from several nearby towns and even had a bus service that replaced a town trolley in the forties. Those trolley tracks still ran down the center of Front Street and joined with numerous cross streets. My father used to thrill my brother and me by mounting his old Plymouth on those tracks and letting those steel ribbons steer us around a curve. "See, kids, no hands!"

Change was coming to this pleasant city of tree-lined streets during the fifties and sixties. A black migration from the southern states, together with more and more whites moving out to the suburban areas of Morris, Somerset, and Hunterdon counties, brought about a shift in Plainfield's racial composition. That same trend was true of just about all the urban municipalities in northern and central New Jersey. Those same homes in the West End that were the pride of the factory worker of the forties and fifties were now inhabited by African Americans, many of whom relied on welfare benefits to survive. All the factories either closed or relocated, so jobs were scarce. Life in the poverty-stricken West End was not easy, as the economic base of wage earners diminished.

The matriarchal society that the black community had become gave rise to the average family financial provider being a middle-aged woman who not only brought home the bacon, but also handled the child-rearing. Many of these working women served as maids and nannies for the more affluent. Working-age men lucky enough to be hired off a street corner for a day's labor were the exception rather than the rule. Many black men, therefore, had too much time on their hands, as well as understandably injured pride. Drug and alcohol abuse was rampant in Plainfield in those years. All this served as the backdrop for the beginning of my eight-year law enforcement career.

During my childhood in the late forties and throughout the fifties, I had no inkling that I would someday become a member of the Plainfield Police Department. When I was twelve years old, however, our paths did cross. My family lived just outside the western boundary of Plainfield in the Arbor section of Piscataway Township. In fact, we had a Plainfield mailing address and considered ourselves "Plainfielders" in every way. It was during those years when a carnival, "The World of Mirth," set up its tents just four blocks away from our neighborhood.

My father, a cautious man, warned me: "Pete," he said, using my nickname, "I want you to stay away from the carnival. I know your paper route takes you right past there. I'm concerned about some of the characters that hang around those places. Got it?"

"Okay, Dad."

Well, all I had to do the next day was ride my new red Schwinn up to the front of the carnival, and I was hooked. The bright colors, the hurdy-gurdy music, and the hubbub of activity lured me in. I parked my bike with its canvas bag stuffed full of *Courier News* papers all neatly folded and through the turnstile I went. Over the next hour I walked around in amazement and even won a teddy bear, which I gave to one of my neighbors, Carol Acker. I couldn't bring it home, could I?

When I went back for my bike, it was gone and my papers were blowing all over the lot. I was crushed. I tearfully walked the rest of my paper route trying to come up with a story for my father, but I knew that no amount of creativity would work.

He saw me walking down the street sans the bike. "You went to the carnival and your bike was stolen," he said, nodding his head slowly. How could he know all that just from seeing me walking down the street? Parents of twelve year olds just know.

My father reported the theft to the Plainfield Police, and I walked my route the next several days. I suppose Dad thought the loss of the bike and his lecture were punishment enough.

Out of the blue, a phone call from the Plainfield Police dispatcher brightened our day. It seemed that an alert Officer Ernest Smalko spotted the spanking-new bright red Schwinn dumped in a local cemetery on Plainfield Avenue and took a closer look. His reaction probably went like this: "Yup, red Schwinn, same serial number. Checks out. Some kid must have needed a ride home and 'borrowed' it."

When Officer Smalko pulled up to our house with my bike sticking out of the police car trunk, it was tears of joy this time.

Fast-forward almost ten years. The desk lieutenant on duty that night needed someone to fill in for an officer who called in sick. This would be my first night in a radio car with a senior man. As we slowly patrolled up and down and behind the stores on that midnight shift, the officer didn't say much. I guess he wasn't too pleased to be stuck with a rookie as his partner for the night. He did his grouchy best whenever he spoke.

"Open that window and keep it open. How do you expect to hear glass breaking with it shut?"

After a while, tiring of the cold shoulder—that is, mostly my right shoulder from the open window, but his cold shoulder, as well—I leaned over and quietly said, "Thanks!"

Somewhat taken back, he said, "What for?"

"Thanks for bringing me back my bike, Officer Smalko. You were my hero for the longest time. Every time I looked at that Schwinn, I remembered you pulling it out of the police car and lecturing me on following orders. I still remember the serial number."

He smiled, the chill broken, and from then on I was allowed to have my window halfway up. A small victory, but a victory nevertheless.

We Were in Transition, Too

As for us, the lowly recruits, my buddy Bruce Tymeson was an Elvis Presley look-alike. Bruce's mannerisms mimicked old swivel-hips Presley, too. Back home from a three-year stint in the Marine Corps, he fancied himself quite the lover. He had several "close calls" with young ladies before his marriage to Connie. His father sold boats and operated a marina in northern New Jersey, and Bruce, ever the daredevil, raced boats on the Hudson River every summer. He seemed most proud of his false front tooth, which he could protrude outward with a push of his tongue. "Got that knocked out in boot camp. Marines are tough!"

My best man, Bruce, after just seven years on the job, took Connie and their five kids to Anna Maria Island on Florida's gulf coast, where he became chief of police of that small department. He later divorced Connie, and, true to his lover-boy ways, took off with another woman. Forty years later, when we last spoke, Bruce was living in New Hampshire, and his second wife was ill. He was in no mood to reminisce about the "good old days in Plainfield." People don't change much and time takes its toll.

Skippy Saunderson, the third in our rookie trio, had the sharp, angular facial features and the physique of actor Daniel Craig (think *Casino Royale* or *The Girl with the Dragon Tattoo*). At the time, Skippy seemed a bit out of character as a cop. He was anything but responsible back then. We three had to report to HQ daily at 8:00 a.m. during training, and most mornings Bruce and I would drag Skippy out of bed to get him to work on time. He was a loner and didn't talk much about family. The dingy little apartment he called home was just a block from the old police headquarters, and he took meals in Roro's, the poor man's restaurant downstairs. Skippy had a tough exterior, but I always felt a little sorry for him. From the little he shared about himself, I could see that he didn't have much of a childhood. He had little use for his mother and never even mentioned his father. Like Bruce, he was ex-military, having served in the army stationed in Germany as a military policeman.

A little quirky, Skippy was always posing. Hips uneven with one leg askew, he exuded cool. Then there were those loose false teeth that he clenched together when he smiled.

Over the years, Skippy Saunderson would mature in the job to become a detective captain before packing it in and buying a bar in Lake Placid, New York, fortuitously just before the 1980 Winter Olympics. He spent twenty years on the Plainfield PD and, to his credit, was respected by those who worked for him. They said he always stuck up for his men. I was surprised when Skippy got married. The quintessential abrasive wise guy, he had a perpetual chip on his shoulder. I could never see him in a sharing relationship. Forty years later when I tried to rekindle with him, I learned he and his wife, Agnes, had divorced but remained friends. Skippy hadn't changed. He was the same old sandpaper with an overconfident attitude.

BLACK MEN AND WHITE COPS

An undercurrent of mutual fear exists between the police and many in the black community, originating from the country's racial history and leftover repressive social attitudes. Of course, times have changed since the sixties, but even today those still anchored in the ghetto don't see much progress. For the police, the job requires being on the street, outnumbered, often alone in a hostile atmosphere.

The beat cop has always been closest to social life on the streets. With enough interaction, racial barriers begin to fade. In law-enforcement terms, it's called "community policing." Even in the early sixties when racial tensions were highest, law-abiding blacks appreciated the police presence on the street. We were literally the difference between life and death for some. We calmed domestic disputes. We arrested burglars, murderers, and rapists and otherwise did our best to make it safe for families to survive in what can only be described as marginal living circumstances.

New officers would have to earn their "street cred." In the community's eyes, you were either fair and firm or nasty and bigoted—one or the other. There were, of course, the unreasonable few who hated the police no matter what. Dealing with the latter was simple: do what you are hired to do and protect yourself at all times. The bottom line was to give and demand respect, but always display confidence.

Lieutenant Campbell said it best: "Police work is 90 percent bluff and 10 percent follow-through." Most times police partners are outnumbered by dozens, if not hundreds, to one. Inasmuch as each officer represents the law and civil authority, most people at the scene of an incident usually restrain themselves from attacking the officers, as much as some might want to. That self-restraint stems from being singled out and the fear of reprisal by the legal system. The outcome of that balancing act is dependent on just how officers carry themselves in the moment. Some get it; some don't.

Many times while in uniform, my partner and I would walk into an all-black bar late on a weekend night looking to serve an arrest warrant or having been summoned by the owner. The joint was run down, smoke-filled, dark, and crowded with black men leaning on the bar. As soon as we would enter, the place quieted and all attention was on us, the hate stare palpable. It was important to take care of business and get out before trouble had a chance to bubble over. All it would take was one act of foolish bravado on either side, and we could be in deep trouble.

FEAR—GET OVER IT

Bob Giaretta was the toughest kid in my elementary school class. Tall, thin, and sinewy with penetrating black eyes, he had a wicked bolo punch that put many a kid flat on his back on Arbor School's playground. He wasn't a bully. He just didn't take any crap from anybody, and everybody knew it, even the older kids.

About ten years after witnessing one of Bob's victims hit the dirt, I was summoned, along with my radio-car partner, to a small bar on West Third Street in Plainfield to take an unruly patron into custody. As it happens, Bob Giaretta and his dad owned the place. From behind the bar, he was surprised to see me. After booking the miscreant, we returned to the bar to get the details for our report.

Bob said, "Boy, Watts, I wouldn't do your job for all

the tea in China. What you do is really dangerous!" It was an ego boost hearing that from Bob. Imagine me, the kid voted "friendliest," and far from the toughest, in my high school graduating class taking the bad guy out in front of rough-and-tumble Bob Giaretta.

Being fearful doesn't make you a sissy. Common sense tells us that fear serves us well. Would you be a "fraidycat" to avoid a tornado or a poisonous snake? There is not a single military veteran who would deny experiencing fear before, during, and after combat. It's that little light bulb that goes off in your brain and says, "Hey, dummy, you'd better wake up and watch your step here!" That's your inner homo sapiens signaling a fight-or-flight alert.

However, fear can be managed, channeled, and overcome. President Theodore Roosevelt was a sickly child growing up, but his father made him face up to his everyday fears. Roosevelt, believing he should make it on his own, went out West and lived among cattle ranchers. He described his experiences this way: "There were all kinds of things I was afraid of at first, ranging from grizzly bears to 'mean' horses and gunfighters, but by acting as if I was not afraid, I gradually ceased to be afraid." Several decades later, another Roosevelt rallied our nation by saying, "We have nothing to fear but fear itself!"

I mention all this because handling fear is a major component in law enforcement. Really. While most officers avoid the conversation, all experience fear. When I first took to the streets in my new uniform, I found myself, like Teddy Roosevelt, *acting* unafraid, while on the inside fear lurked. Again, like Teddy, as time went on I was able to set aside and actually overcome fear. In fact, after just a few months into the job, I found something in myself I had not recognized previously. I really could handle myself both physically and mentally in all kinds of situations. It just took the doing-of-it to come to the knowing-of-it. In short, we need to be put into some circumstances to understand our own capabilities. Maybe it takes looking back fifty years to be able to admit all this and put it in perspective.

FITTING IN—AWKWARD

I was pretty skinny back when I was first starting in law enforcement, and I wore my hat in a fifty-mission crush style with the brim so low on my forehead I had to lift my head to see the horizon. I must admit I was quite taken with myself in my new role as a law-enforcement officer. Until then, I had not had much worldly experience. Working for Lockheed Engineering in the cost-accounting department and one year of Rutgers night school had not prepared me for much of anything. That I now had a real job and was on a course toward a real career was important to me.

Foolishly, however, I felt indestructible, as did my colleagues, Bruce and Skippy. The truth is, we were just impressionable youngsters and every day was an adventure. As with most in their early twenties, we lived in the moment. I looked forward to donning the uniform and going to work every day. I loved it. I often commented to family and friends, "I would even do this for no pay if I could survive financially."

But police work tends to bring life into focus a bit more demonstrably, often in life-or-death circumstances. Naïveté tends to wilt away at a murder scene, a fatal auto accident, a race riot, or even a nasty domestic quarrel. It's called *life experience*, and the gloomier visions do grow on you. The trick is not to let the darker side of humanity, found abundantly in police work, alter you as a person. Witnessing life at the bottom of the human food chain, the norm in law enforcement, is an education I would not have missed for anything. It has made me grateful for every day I spend on this earth. And I have never let it contaminate my outlook. I am still the "friendliest kid in school."

Although I didn't know it then, I was becoming something of a maverick. Sergeant Reilly called me on the radio one night and ordered me to ticket a whole row of cars parked illegally in front of a house party in the south end of the city. I arrived a few minutes later and, instead of writing them up, I warned some folks to move their cars. Some did; some didn't. An hour passed and Reilly got all over my case for not writing up those remaining cars. I went back and wrote the tickets. You didn't mess with Reilly, one of the more serious-natured patrol sergeants.

The next day in the locker room at shapeup, Patrolman Ray Evans came up to me at the pool table in a menacing way and said, "You gave my friends tickets last night, and I don't appreciate it!" This was in front of the whole four-to-midnight crew about to go on duty. Ray, a chubby black officer, had a strange way of twisting his head around when he talked, leaning forward with wild, bulging eyes. Everybody pretty much left Ray alone. That same act worked for him on the street, too.

I explained, "Hey, Ray, Reilly sent me there and got pissed when I only gave 'em warnings. Some just didn't listen, so I had to write 'em up. Sorry 'bout that."

"Don't give me that crap, Watts. You don't have to give anybody a ticket that you don't want to. You young punks try to set the world on fire." As he walked away, he threw in over his shoulder, "Remember, you still have to join the PBA!"

The insinuation was clear. New officers, after six months on the job, become eligible to apply for membership in the Patrolmen's Benevolent Association. This face-to-face confrontation and his implication was one that I could not let pass. Losing the respect of fellow officers is not good for a rookie, so right after his not-so-veiled PBA threat, I shot back, "I don't *have* to join anything!" My comeback did not conform to Ray's subservient image of what a rookie officer should be, and his facial expression made it clear this was not over.

Evans got under my skin, and my independent side bubbled over. Just a few months on the job and I was getting off on the wrong foot, through no fault of my own. My response to Evans spread through the department and, of course, was embellished with each telling. By the time

I was eligible, what with the scuttlebutt circulating about me, I wasn't sure I wanted to join the PBA at all. Several of the more reasonable officers, however, convinced me to go ahead with my application, suggesting that I shouldn't let a few bad apples determine my future. So I put in the application and was approved by just one vote.

Amusingly, a few years later, I took a Wednesday off from my detective duties, which was the day of the regular monthly PBA meeting. The bad apples were lying in wait. Not having attended the meeting, as was expected on my day off, I got a letter from the PBA advising that I owed a one-dollar fine. My quick response was a letter of resignation from the PBA with concise anatomical instructions as to where they could put their letter and the enclosed dollar.

HUP, TWO, THREE, FOUR

About a year into my job with the Plainfield Police, the draft board decided my presence was required elsewhere. I was off to basic training just one month after my marriage to Linda in May 1962, then off to a two-year New England "honeymoon" courtesy of the U.S. Army. Although my police experience was limited to just one year, the army saw fit to make me a military policeman without going to M.P. school. My duty station was formally known as United States Army, Natick Laboratories Annex, Sudbury, Massachusetts, or USANLASM, as it was affectionately dubbed by post inhabitants.

When I received my orders after eight weeks of basic training at Fort Dix, they contained specific instructions to show up at your new posting without your car, your wife, or anything else you might want to take along. Linda and I talked about it.

"Let's see," I said. "Massachusetts is just a five-hour drive away, so let's load up and take what we want. If they won't allow you to stay, you can always just drive back and stay with your mother." So, we loaded up the 1954 Mercury with clothes, television, pots and pans, and whatever else we could fit into it and landed at the Shamrock Motel on Route 9 in Framingham, Massachusetts. Then came the moment of truth: reporting to the main base in Natick.

Linda nervously waited in the Merc while I tentatively walked under a sign that read, "Company HQ – Orderly Room." I reported to a portly sergeant in his fifties. This big bald blob was perched behind his desk, a short stogie clenched in his teeth. He looked like a no-nonsense kind of guy, and any hope for my new bride staying with me was beginning to fade.

I saluted smartly and announced, "Private Watts reporting for duty, Sergeant," to which he barked, "Son, you don't salute sergeants. Didn't you learn anything in basic?"

This was not going well. Reviewing my file while tapping his pencil, he said, "So . . . did you bring your wife with you?" *That's it*, I thought. *Bye-bye, Linda.*

"Yes, I did, Sergeant." Defeat was imminent.

"Good," he said. "We have no room to billet

you anywhere, so you're gonna have to find a place off-post." He spat out the stogie, picked up his phone, and instructed his orderly, "A Private Watts is going to get with you in a couple of minutes. Give him a seventy dollar off-post advance, a three-day pass, and driving instructions to the Sudbury base." The sergeant turned to me, smiled, and said, "Welcome to the army, son. Buy a local paper and find a place to flop. We take care our own." Lesson learned: blobs that bark will not necessarily bite.

My rural Sudbury posting was actually three thousand acres of woods with about fifty grass-camouflaged bunkers, each serviced by railroad tracks. The army stored everything from quartermaster clothing to Nike surface-to-air missiles in those bunkers. The military police on the base were charged with normal police duties, as well as post security, especially watchful for those bunkers. Platoon Sergeant Vincent Della Jacono was the immediate supervisor of our small M.P. unit consisting of about twenty draftees like myself.

"Della" was a dark Italian guy in his mid-thirties from Brooklyn and was married to a petite Japanese woman he met while stationed over there. He was about six feet tall with a square jaw and lots of black hair that flowed from everywhere his uniform didn't cover. He had to shave twice a day. Della was a career soldier, and we all respected him. He was fair and had served just about everywhere in Europe and Asia by the time he inherited our bunch.

Mostly we patrolled the base, which included the

perimeter road inside a high fence and going outside the main gate to check periodically on the Raytheon facility about two miles into the woods across the main road. One late night Private Rice, a short black kid from Detroit, and I checked on Raytheon only to find a laboratory building alarm going off. It was really loud, but because the building was so far back from the main road, no one could hear it without driving down the two-mile drive to get there.

Our first thought was an intruder. I told Rice to go around the back, and I would go in using the key to check it out. He refused, stood closer to me, and said, "Watts, ain't no way I'm going back there in the dark." Okay, so we both went in the front, our .45s leading the way.

With the alarm drilling into our brains, we looked around inside. The lab looked much like any other lab I had seen, but bigger. There was at least a half-acre of shiny metal benches with sinks topped with all kinds of weird rigging. There was no obvious sign of a burglary and no getaway car nearby, so my focus switched to this being a possible fire alarm going off.

"Only one way to find out," I said. I went over to the wall and pulled the fire alarm box. The first alarm was now joined by another, only louder. Rice hollered over the din, "Holy shit! The base fire department must be hooked into this."

I ran back to the M.P. truck and radioed to the guard shack that this was a false alarm and that I had just pulled the hook. This all took place at around three a.m., so except for our M.P. shift and the overnight orderly in the first sergeant's office, all on the base were asleep. We learned later that the base fire department came to life when the alarm sounded. The overhead bay doors went up and the fire engines were pulled out onto the apron while waiting for the rest of the firemen to mount up. Then suddenly everything stopped. The trucks backed in, the doors came down, the lights went out, and all returned to the stillness of the night. The M.P. in our guard shack, of course, relayed my message that it was a false alarm.

Sergeant Della Jacono was not pleased with my "field decision" to test the fire alarm, which earned me permanent midnight shift for the next month. While he understood my rationale, he said that I should have called him instead of bringing the whole base to life at that hour. He also said there were a few, especially in the fire department, who wanted my head, so I was okay with Della's decision to get me out of sight for a while. My presence in the daytime chow line would not have been a pleasant experience.

I know you are waiting to hear why the alarm had gone off in the first place. It was set to ring when the humidity inside the building exceeded the prescribed limit. Live and learn—I've done a lot of that and often the hard way.

Later during my two-year tour, a local policeman in the adjoining small town of Maynard was shot during a traffic stop. The shooter climbed the fence and disappeared into the remote wooded area of our army base. Our M.P.

unit was activated and search sectors were assigned. Della said, "Watts, you come with me." On the way out to the M.P. patrol truck, he confided, "Let those inexperienced kids patrol the perimeter." Della knew I had been a cop in civilian life. "You and I will go where I think the action will be. He's gotta get in from the cold, so let's check the outbuildings first." That comment led me to believe I was back in Della's good graces after the fire alarm business. Right away we found a building with an unlocked front door. We went in carefully, but Della couldn't resist whispering, "You go to the right, but try to stay away from the fire alarm."

It took two days and a state police helicopter to run that felon down, and Della was in on the capture. Vincent Della Jacono was a good man, whom I considered to be a mentor in my early years. He later went to Vietnam, survived, retired, and took a position in a New York law firm as the office manager. Retired military are ideal office managers, just so you know.

As military people, Linda and I were not exactly enthusiastic about life in Massachusetts. The sign in front of a house in the nearby town of Maynard read, "Dogs and soldiers keep off the lawn!" Strange welcome wagon, no? We lived off-post, and later in my hitch we both had part-time jobs so we could stay together.

We found a small cottage close enough to the army base. It had a propane-tank hot-air heating system that cost us more each month in the winter than the rent, but it was newly renovated, clean, and cute with a knotty-pine kitchenette. One month we ran out of money early with no food in the cupboard, just hot dogs and peanut butter with two weeks until payday. I had a three-day pass from my military police duties, so I told Linda, "I'm taking the car and looking for work. We only have a quarter tank of gas, so if I'm not back by noon, you'll know I found something."

I went from farm to farm in this rural Massachusetts countryside offering to muck out stalls or anything else that needed doing. Getting low on gas, I stopped in a station to buy some, which was only 28.9 cents a gallon at the time, when I had another idea. I went up to the owner and asked if he had anything I could do. Leaning back, he looked me up and down from behind his cluttered and grease-stained metal desk.

"Army?" he asked, apparently recognizing my fatigue pants and beat-up combat boots.

"Yeah, we need help pretty bad. My wife is here with me and I could sure use some work so we can stay together."

Stiffly rising from his seat, he said, "I served in Korea. Got some nasty work in the back. Think you're up for it?" His tobacco-stained teeth presenting a yellowed but genuine smile, he continued, "Know what truck split rims are?"

I didn't, but learned quickly and painfully. To get those big truck tires off their rims, you have to use a sledgehammer and two metal bars. You wedge the bars just right between the rim and the tire to separate them. It helps to get one of the bars started and hold it down with your foot while you wrestle the other one in the opposite direction. This was a job no one wanted, but I was glad for it. As far as I was concerned, this big pile of truck tires had been sitting there waiting for me. Despite some bloody fingers and a sore back, I knocked off half of them by the time the boss was ready to close about six hours later.

"Good going, kid. Can you come back tomorrow?"

"Yeah, I can . . . but . . . uh . . . ya see, uh."

"I get it. You want to be paid for today, right?"

When I put that twenty-dollar bill down on the kitchen counter back at the cottage, Linda and I both cried. This meant that we could make it until I got my army pay and Linda's allotment check. More importantly, it meant Linda would not have to go back to New Jersey. We went to an IGA supermarket in Marlboro and spent thirteen dollars on groceries, which bought a lot in those days, and we even put a couple more bucks of gas in the old Mercury. I never forgot that gas station man and his compassion for a fellow soldier. Over the years, there have been many whom I thank for the opportunity to get ahead or even survive. We made it on our own, for sure; but working hard, viewing the future optimistically, and seizing on opportunities has proven to be life's best path. Bemoaning the present never changes the future.

We were to face other tough times. Once we got out of the service, we couldn't buy a home because it required a hefty down payment. My police salary didn't amount to much, so we rented. Sure, we didn't relish the predicament we were in, but we vowed to stick it out no matter what hard times came along. It took us twelve years of renting before we had our own home. Now, in our fifty-third year together, we know that those early years of struggle forged the inner strength to handle just about anything that comes our way.

"Kachunk, Kachunk"

Until that Saturday afternoon on Rushmore Avenue waiting for Howard Swint's arrival with Lieutenant Hennessey, I generally walked a beat downtown. I was also assigned as a replacement in a patrol car when one of the senior guys had a day off. The real action, of course, was in the patrol car, especially at night. Our two-man cars would cover accidents, domestic disputes, burglaries, and anything else that came along. However, beginners like me spent a fair amount of time on a walking beat.

There is nothing as lonely as a walking beat on the midnight shift. In those days we had no portable radios or cell phones to keep us in touch with the rest of the world. I had this big brass key dangling on my belt that opened a green callbox on a telephone pole that was a direct landline to the desk lieutenant. Those green boxes had a lever that the beat cop triggered hourly on different corners. That was just to let the lieutenant know I was still breathing. Up and down dimly lit streets and the even darker back alleys of those businesses I trudged, ever on the alert. All the while I could hear the traffic lights talking to each other, "Kachunk, kachunk." Now and then the patrol sergeant would cruise by, nod his head, and drive on.

Door shaking was part of the walking beat routine. Front and back doors of all business establishments had to be checked by hand. Every now and then a storeowner would forget to lock up and the door would fly open in my hand. At zero-dark-thirty, let me tell you, that's a heart-stopping sensation. Sometimes interruptions in the monotony were more serious. Once I caught a couple of would-be young burglars behind Rosenbaum's department store in a dark alley. I proudly marched them at gunpoint out to the callbox, and a few minutes later a patrol car showed up and we all went to headquarters. It turned out that I had gone to school with the older brother of one of them. Small world.

Another time I walked down a dark L-shaped alley in the rear of the stores on Front Street, and as I rounded a corner with my flashlight leading the way, a figure suddenly appeared flashing a light back at me. A storeowner had put a large mirror out in the alley at just the right angle. I almost shot that guy.

Bob Miller, one of the more experienced cops, walked a night beat—his preference. He found a back door unlocked one night in a small department store. He went in and called the dispatcher from the store phone and waited for the owner to show up. Normal procedure. The cop from the adjoining walking beat came over, as did the patrol sergeant with coffee and doughnuts all around while waiting for the owner to show. Well, as cops do, the war stories flowed. To illustrate a point during one of his tall tales, Bob kicked a nearby clothes kiosk saying, "Okay, come out of there, you sonavabitch!" It was part of Bob's story dialogue; but lo and behold, a terrified voice from below screamed, "Don't shoot. I'm coming out."

The would-be burglar surrendered, as Bob and the others coughed up coffee and doughnuts all over themselves.

"Officer, I'm Going to Make You Famous!"

My weirdest walking-beat recollection begins one chilly early morning while standing near the callbox at Watchung Avenue and East Front Street, watching the minute hand get closer to my ring time. Heavy rain made visibility poor, but at 5:45 a.m., there wasn't much to see, anyway. I was completely covered with twenty-pounds of black rubber raincoat and boots, which included a black cape over my hat. As I stood there dripping, my gaze wandered up Watchung Avenue toward North Plainfield.

A lone figure was walking toward me under an umbrella. That the man would be out walking in this weather and at this time of day was odd enough, but what followed was even more bizarre. As he sloshed along, head down and umbrella overhead, I could see he had a large book clutched tightly to his chest. When he came to the curb at Front Street, he looked up and saw me. His eyes brightened and he hustled across the intersection, coming toward me with a cheery, "Good morning, Officer. You are going to become famous today."

"How's that?" I asked.

"I am going to make you famous. You have just discovered the long-lost Lindbergh baby."

A blank stare conveyed my apparent disbelief, because he repeated it. "That's right. I am Baby Lindbergh."

He handed me the umbrella and opened a thick scrapbook, carefully shielding his treasure against the rain. There was nothing threatening about him, so I went along with it. I studied him for a moment while he flipped pages: This guy was in his forties, well groomed, and friendly enough. Unless he intended to bring an umbrella to a gunfight, I didn't see any reason to be concerned about my safety, though he stood uncomfortably close to me. He began leafing through various pages of the scrapbook, showing me photos of himself and comparing them to photos of Charles Lindbergh and the lost child.

"See the ears, the nose? There's no doubt they're the same person." He pointed to a photo of the child, straightened up, and proudly proclaimed, "That's me."

Surmising that I had a deranged person on my hands (duh?), right here in the middle of this early morning downpour, I schmoozed him. "My lieutenant should see this evidence, so that your true identify can be told." I then thought, *Wow, it would have to be Scotty on duty. He'll bite my head off. I wonder if he finished off his ice cream yet.*

Lieutenant David Scott answered my callbox ring with, "Waddaya want, Watts? This better be good." This was the quiet time on the midnight shift, and the dispatcher and desk officer would often take turns with brief snoozes. I couldn't resist it. "Lieutenant, we're gonna be famous. You and I just discovered the long-lost Lindbergh baby." My umbrella companion, staring at the puddles forming around his shoes, nodded his head, affirming my every word.

Lieutenant Scott, on the other hand, spouted a few deleted expletives and asked if I had been drinking. Every time he took a breath between outbursts, I was able to squeeze in enough to convince Scottie to send a radio car to pick up "Baby Lindbergh."

It turns out the man was a patient at Lyons Veterans Hospital who just up and walked out of one of the dorms. He hitched a ride with a bakery truck and walked through North Plainfield from Route 22 looking for someone to convince of his real identity. Police work brings one into contact with everyone from the rich to the poor and, yes, the hopelessly lost, too.

Let's Not Scramble Any Eggs!

Several years later, I was riding as senior officer with George Lane, a recruit, as my partner. We got a radio call to meet a Mrs. Robinson at an address in the west end of town. The dispatcher said she was having some trouble with her grandson, Albert. When we arrived, an elderly black lady met us at the end of the driveway of a two-and-a-half-story single-family home. A very agitated Mrs. Robinson tearfully explained, "My grandson hasn't been taking his medicine and is acting crazy. He is in the kitchen and I am afraid to go in there."

George and I went quietly through the front door with Mrs. Robinson close behind, still babbling on about Albert being a good boy, but with some problems. I shushed her so we could see what was going on without upsetting Albert. I did a quick peek from the dining room into the kitchen.

There stood a tall black man in his twenties with a vacant stare on his face. He was up against the front of the stove breaking eggs into a frying pan held in his left oven-mitted hand. In that second I saw hot grease bubbling over onto the stovetop. Albert was in another zone, making for a dangerous and unpredictable situation in the form of a pan full of hot grease and at least a dozen eggs bubbling in the caldron.

We huddled together in the hall and I came up with a plan. There was no way we were going to go into the kitchen to try to talk to Albert. It's one thing to arrest and cuff somebody, but adding a pan of hot grease to the equation is reason to pause and think this out.

"Mrs. Robertson, do you think you can get Albert to come into the dining room?"

"I can try."

At this point, Albert did not know we were there. Albert probably didn't know where Albert was, so I thought surprise was in our favor. I put George on one side of the doorway, and I took the other with Mrs. Robinson in plain view for Albert to see. I told George that the only thing we should concentrate on was that frying pan and getting control over it before Albert could act against us with it. I nodded to Mrs. Robinson.

"Albert, look what I found upstairs," Mrs. Robinson hollered. "You ain't gonna believe this!"

Albert came through the doorway with the sizzling frying pan held in one gloved hand and a dishtowel wrapped around the handle in the other. George and I grabbed both his wrists at the same time and firmly steered him toward a nearby coffee table.

I shouted in Albert's right ear, "Put it down!" We took control so suddenly that Albert had no time to react. Thankfully, he released the frying pan onto the table. Often, the key to defusing a potentially dangerous situation is taking control early and decisively.

We cuffed Albert and took him to the psychiatric section of Muhlenberg Hospital along with a much-relieved Mrs. Robinson.

I was involved in many more such incidents while I was in uniform. The allure to patrol work was that when you began your shift, you never knew what you would be involved in before it was over.

WHAT A BRAVE, BIG BOY!

When I got back from the army, Plainfield had changed to one-man cars. Instead of the old three district two-man patrol cars, we now had eight cars out on each shift with specific patrol areas. Some officers didn't like it because there was a lack of security patrolling alone. On the other hand, we offered the public quicker response times. Everyone was happier when the chief allowed a second car to go on a call or to a pulled-over motorist; thus, backup was just a moment away. Two minutes was the average arrival time for an emergency call. It was greeted favorably by the public, and the officers got used to it in time.

I was patrolling alone in the south end of Plainfield near Muhlenberg Hospital one late afternoon when I got a call about an injured child. There are two types of calls where responding officers go all out. They are: "Officer needs assistance" and "Injured child."

I took off down Randolph Road with overhead lights on and siren blaring. This was a residential neighborhood, but the street was pretty wide and there was no other traffic, so I really poured it on. Suddenly, I spotted a car tire lying flat right in the middle of the road ahead of me. At this speed I couldn't avoid it without losing control and I was going too fast to stop. All I could think of was *I hope to Hell there is no rim in that damned tire!* As the patrol car flew over the tire, there was a momentary rumbling sound as the tire was gobbled up in the undercarriage and then exploded out the back. No rim, thank God! A quick glance in the rearview mirror caught it bouncing up and down on the blacktop. That was the night I realized it was better to get where I was going safely than a few seconds earlier.

When I got to the injured boy, I found him sitting underneath a swing set with a deep gash in his calf. Surprisingly, there was not much bleeding, but his calf muscle and some tendons were exposed. His mother was frantic. When this five-year-old saw me, his face lit up. He was more enthralled with the policeman coming to his rescue than he was concerned about his injury. As I got out of the car, I popped the trunk and grabbed the first aid kit. His mom couldn't believe how fast I got there. "I just called a minute ago," she said. I wondered if that tire was still bouncing along Randolph Road and just smiled—again thankful there was no rim inside the tire.

I began applying a bandage tightly to protect the wound from the elements. I told him not to look at it and commented, "What a brave, big boy you are. So, little man, how did you manage to do this?"

"I tried to do a back flip off the seat, but my leg got caught on that thing." He pointed at a bolt sticking out of the framework that held the swing set together.

Shortly thereafter, the rescue squad took over and my job was done. Many of the other emergency calls I handled did not end as well. Sometimes people died or were already dead from heart attacks or auto accidents, and there were several train incidents with body parts spread over a quarter-mile length of tracks. Life's realities have a way of undermining the naïvety of inexperience.

Uniform policing entails anything that comes your way. That's what makes it so challenging and rewarding. Then again, as retired New Jersey State Police Major Bill Baum puts it, "A career in uniform policing is one year's experience twenty times." But I was not destined to remain in uniform for much longer, and Lieutenant Dan Hennessey was about to make that happen.

CHAPTER TWO

"There He Goes!"

Back on Rushmore Avenue, we had been sitting in Hennessey's Dodge for about twenty minutes—not talking much, just sitting there, eyes fixed on the green Pontiac. Whenever I snuck a peek his way, Hennessey was stoically staring straight ahead. I suppose our relative age, rank, and experience level explained it, but the silence was palpable. *What can I say that would actually interest him? I'm being too sensitive—just wait. Just be cool.* If you ask Linda, she will tell you I was never one for putting up with too much silence.

Lieutenant Detective Dan Hennessey was a slightly built man with a sallow complexion and thinning brown hair he combed straight back over the top. He had a weak chin, his eyes bulged a little, and he had a shaky, nervous way about him. But his physical appearance belied the man underneath. Dan was in his early forties and had a reputation as a tough straight shooter. "Honest as the day is long," they said. That is why he was chosen to head up a new unit in the department devoted to gambling, narcotics, and other vices. The worst they could come up with against Hennessey was that he lied about his age to join the U.S. Navy when WWII broke out. He went in at fifteen and came out four years later when most his age then were being drafted.

There had been a couple of detective sergeants in charge of vice, but their reputations were ruined when a Union County grand jury brought back a presentment against the City of Plainfield and its police department.

Presentment is a term you don't hear much. The usual function of a grand jury is to take in evidence supplied by law enforcement and the prosecutor with an indictment and criminal charges in mind; but grand juries also render presentments. When a grand-jury investigation determines that a governmental body or employees thereof have acted improperly, yet not to the extent that criminality can likely be proven, a presentment may be offered to the court in jurisdiction. The Plainfield presentment was, in essence, a severe public rebuke of the department and those two detectives for their failure to actively pursue gambling violations in the city. It directed that measures be taken to energetically enforce gambling laws in Plainfield. This insinuation of corruption embarrassed the city fathers, as well as the whole department.

Those two detectives were suspected of colluding with organized crime, though no criminal charges were ever brought. The fact that the sister of one was a household servant in the home of a suspected Mafia figure in Livingston, New Jersey, and that the detective and his partner reportedly had visited the guy's mansion made for understandable speculation. Along with their arrogant attitudes, both wore expensive suits, complete with silk socks, pointy shoes, and pinky rings. Oh, and did I say their specific duties in the detective bureau included investigating illegal gambling, narcotics, and other vices? Lacking evidence justifying an indictment, the Union County grand jury did the next best thing by issuing the presentment.

I was away doing my military police thing at the time, but Bruce kept us up-to-date with the local scuttlebutt. The newspapers were full of the goings-on, including *Courier News* photos of those scowling detective sergeants sitting in the front row throughout the local council hearings at Plainfield City Hall. The front façade of the police department and city hall were plastered over the front pages, all of which heaped great shame upon the City of Plainfield.

Breaking our long silence in the Dodge on Rushmore Street, Hennessey said, "So, David, what do you think of surveillance so far?"

"Definitely different," I said too quickly. *What a clueless answer. I could've done better than that.*

Then he dropped the bomb. "How would you like to work for me in the detective bureau? We're puttin' together a new squad to work on gambling and narcotics, and your name came up as one to consider." Hennessey shifted in his seat and turned toward me, his body language indicating the drama was over and we were getting down to business.

"You've got a good arrest record and your bosses appreciate your energy; but I gotta tell you, David, there's another reason to pick you. You were away in the army the past two years and are least likely to have been involved in the recent scandal. In short, you're a safe pick."

Hennessey sourly added, "I only wish I could feel that way about everyone else in the department." Turning his gaze out his window, his voice wistfully drifting off, he said, "We just don't know how deep the corruption has gone. Then there's those who aren't directly involved, who sympathize with the gambling element. It's a fuckin' mess, but, by God, my squad is going to get this city back on track." Melancholy and anger pushed aside, he turned back to me and said, "So, anyway, what do you think?"

Not hesitating at all, I blurted, "Yes, sir, absolutely, count me in!"

Little did I know at that same moment Detective Captain Ernie Phillips was on the phone with my young wife. Phillips told Linda I was being considered for a special job in the bureau and wondered what she thought of it. He cautioned, "Linda, unlike uniformed officers and their shift work, plainclothes detectives work odd hours, so family understanding is essential."

He also warned Linda that some uniformed men are jealous of the detectives and may not even talk to her anymore. Linda's retort was classic Linda: "They don't talk to me now, and I wouldn't introduce most of them to my mother."

Evidently, Phillips appreciated her spunk. I have no

doubt that her frank response contributed to the decision to take me into the detective bureau. It's not that Linda and I disliked most of the officers. We did, however, find some to be arrogant and self-possessed. Then there was that Ray Evans incident: "Remember, Watts, you still have to join the PBA." That PBA clique was not in our happy thoughts.

Throughout all our time together, Linda has always been the one with the best read on people. I have always appreciated her ability to keep us out of trouble and on track. I call her my sea anchor. It doesn't stop the boat or change its direction; rather, it just calms forward motion enough to keep going in the right direction.

Hennessey suddenly stiffened. "He's coming out. Now, watch him closely and tell me what you see."

Binoculars up, I saw Howard Swint appear on the porch and, with his head down, make for the Pontiac at a no-nonsense pace this time. He drove away from us, back down Second Street and out of sight.

"There he goes," I said, squirming a little in my seat. *Why aren't we following him?*

Reading my thoughts, Hennessey said, "He'll make us in a flash if we try tailing him. For now, he doesn't know that we're onto this drop house, and that works to our advantage. We'll keep an eye on this house and be able to ID other players. So, David, tell me what you just saw."

I thought a moment, desperate to impress. Swint had moved faster now, unlike when he arrived. His whole demeanor was at a higher pitch, and I said so.

"Good. What else?"

I thought a moment. "The bag, the bag." I stifled my excitement. "He was carrying a brown paper bag when he came out, not when he went in."

"Right on, David. Now let's get the hell outta here and have a Saturday."

As I trace back my beginnings in the investigative field, that day fifty-some years ago on Rushmore Avenue with Lieutenant Dan Hennessey was a pivotal moment—not that I knew it at the time. I was, of course, very impressed that Hennessey knew just when that numbers runner would arrive, in what car, and that he would be leaving carrying a brown paper bag. But it was the physical act of surveillance itself that would change my world about a decade later. Getting one over on "the bad guy" would always be a high for me. I was hooked. For most of my adult life to come, there would be many "Here he comes, there he goes!" moments. Years later, my career would heavily depend on the ability to conduct surveillance on unsuspecting insurance fraud claimants and corporate cheats.

A "Trickery" Business

Surveillance is a tricky and, if you will, a "trickery" business. Basically, you watch people and their activities without their knowledge. The latter is the trickery part. Blending into surroundings and shielding behind other people or vehicles is the name of the game, along with pulling it off long enough to be there when whatever is suspected of happening actually happens. When "it" goes down, your camera has to be up, running without a lot of shaking and, of course, not noticeable to the subject. Accomplish all this, by the way, without running over those five nuns in a crosswalk.

Obviously, there is a big difference between following criminal actors who are constantly on the lookout for surveillance and unsuspecting citizen insurance claimants or corporates who are not as conscious of their surroundings. True, some insurance claimants are warned by their lawyers to be watchful for investigators, but few can maintain vigilance day after day. Time is the Achilles heel of the insurance claimant, but not for the criminal who lives that life every moment of every day. When law enforcement conducts surveillance, it is often done in stages. That is, the bad guy is picked up where we left him off yesterday, and another leg of the trip is documented toward discovering his destination. This is especially true when following mobsters in gambling cases. Radar seems part of their makeup, making continuous surveillance tough if not impossible. Of course, in major cases multiple radio-equipped vehicles are used, but the average case is a one or two-man exercise.

Watching surveillance segments on television shows always gives us a laugh. The subject drives off, and the two investigators discuss whether to follow or not. Once decided, they jump into their car, start it, turn around, and pull out into traffic. In real life, several seconds is all it takes for two buses, three taxis, and a truck to be between you and your target vehicle. Then you contend with traffic lights, school buses, and the occasional police cruiser parked nearby. Oh, yeah, then there are those five nuns in the crosswalk. Successful surveillance depends on being constantly organized and prepared, anticipating movements of the subject, and advantageous placement of your own vehicle. A little luck helps, too.

Stationary surveillance is ideal. We choose a vantage point close enough to accommodate photography, yet far enough away to be less obvious. We have an excuse ready when a neighbor comes up to the van asking why we are parked in front of his house. "Oh, we are waiting for a real estate agent. I'm not familiar with this area and she told me to wait near this intersection. I'm sorry . . . I'll move if you want." That works, but better is to have magnetic signs made up and traffic cones put out with another story ready. "We're conducting a traffic survey in the area because they are considering a traffic light a couple of blocks up." I can't tell you how many folks in central New Jersey are still waiting for new traffic lights or new sewers.

The police are always curious about strange vehicles in residential neighborhoods and justifiably so. The best policy is to check in with the police before setting up; however, that can lead to problems, too. The subject of the investigation may be friendly with the locals or even be related to an officer, so there is another way. We set up without notifying the police and when a police cruiser comes down the street, we become proactive. We get out, approach him with our identification in hand, and explain that we just followed someone into the area and are waiting for the person to move. As long as the police are satisfied that we are legitimate and not burglars or worse, they will likely go along with us. If a neighbor then reports a strange van in the neighborhood, the police dispatcher lets them know it is sanctioned and not to worry about it.

One misty predawn morning found Linda and me in our van awaiting the appearance of an insurance claimant when a knock came at the side door facing away from the subject's house. I peeked through the curtain and saw a middle-aged guy in casual clothes. He had that "cop look." He held up his New Jersey State Police badge, so I let him in. He appreciated the fact that we were working on an insurance claim but advised that the next-door neighbor to our claimant was a member of the Vito Genovese crime family and his surveillance took precedence over ours. I agreed. We called the insurance company and told them to find another way to mitigate that claim, because surveillance in that neighborhood was out of the question.

Sitting on surveillance takes physical and mental stamina. A minivan is best suited for the job, and a porta-potty is an absolute necessity. When things are about to happen, you can't declare "time out" to take care of personal business. In extreme weather conditions, you can't run the air conditioner or the heater without attracting attention either, so you have to dress accordingly and tough it out.

Hours go by with nothing happening. Then, in the span of a few seconds, the garage door opens and the car backs out and goes up the street and out of sight. You have to be prepared for that moment with everything in the van strategically placed, including people. The difficulty is trying to keep up with the subject without weaving in and out of traffic and quickly choosing a good stopping spot once he has landed. The hardest part is the boredom in between isolated moments of sheer pandemonium. I cannot say it enough: patience, stamina, self-denial, and preparation are absolute requirements for successful surveillance. In spite of all the electronic gimmicks today, those four elements are still essential to surveillance work.

Surveillance while in the detective bureau had its benefits, however. We drove fast, cut others off, and violated red lights, albeit carefully. All this, of course, without worrying about getting a traffic summons. After all, we were the good guys protecting the public from the bad guys. Sometimes we had to go a bit over the line to keep up with those bad guys, so traffic laws seemed secondary.

Another difficulty we had during my early police detective days was equipment. We had no surveillance vans and used our own cars to chase the gamblers and drug dealers around. Our radios were ridiculously large and with limited range. Everything we did, thinking back, was on a wing and a prayer. It is surprising we did as well as we did.

CHAPTER THREE

The Name of the Game: Improvise

The special plainclothes squad of the Plainfield Police Department was small at the time I was a part of it—three of us plus Lieutenant Dan Hennessey. Under his supervision and tutelage we racked up an impressive record of gambling and narcotic arrests, in spite of being undermanned and lacking proper equipment. Hennessey likened our situation to "chasing Caddies with Model Ts." We had a long wish list of equipment but weren't holding our collective breath. As Hennessey used to say, quoting an old Scottish rhyme, "If wishes were horses, beggars would ride. If horse turds were biscuits, they'd eat till they died." Whenever one of us would start bitching about the lack of equipment, the boss would start the first line and we three would chime in with the second line, laugh, and get back to work.

What *was* new and spiffy at the time, however, was police headquarters. The city bought a whole block of stores at the corner of West Fourth Street and Watchung Avenue, which included the old roller rink, and put up the new building. A new era began. Our squad was located on the second floor at the far end of the spanking-new detective bureau. A wall separated us from the rest of the bureau, and our files were locked up at all times. It was by nature a secretive operation.

We kept meticulous records of every observation we made on the street, and once we had enough information, we used that data to obtain a search warrant. There were times we had to sneak up the back stairs to Municipal Judge Irving Kunzman's private law firm to present our affidavit. This was because the elevator operator was a player and, no doubt, would have put the word out on the street that a search warrant was in the works. All action would have stopped in Plainfield for that day and our raid would've been for naught. The judge took a liking to our squad and did all he could to help us refine our paperwork. He even put up with us bothering him at home when necessary.

I did, however, get into trouble with Judge Kunzman once. Freddie and I arrested a small-time drug dealer who was represented by attorney Norman Abrams, one of Plainfield's better criminal defense lawyers. He filed a motion to suppress evidence on the basis of an illegal search. We testified that we saw the marijuana in plain sight, but Abrams managed to convince Judge Kunzman that we could not have known it was marijuana in the "shiny glassine envelopes" until we opened them. The judge ruled the evidence was obtained improperly and granted Abrams's motion. That meant the evidence could not be used in the trial, resulting in the case being thrown out. During a slight pause in the proceedings, I stood up in the audience.

"Excuse me, Judge, does that mean I have to give him back his pot?"

Judge Kunzman's jaw dropped. "In my chambers, Watts, and bring your lieutenant!"

I got a good ass-chewing that day. Afterward, Lieutenant Hennessey said I really had to learn when to pick a fight and when to walk away. That time my maverick side lost the battle, but the lesson wasn't lost on me.

Sometimes we had to take extra care before a raid. Hennessey would go to city hall to check the tax rolls—remember, there was no Internet back then. When you raid someone's house, you want to be 100 percent sure it is the right house and that the occupants are the subjects of the raid. Busting into the wrong house was a lawsuit in the making, even back in the sixties. Hennessey couldn't check on the subject's house without raising suspicions, so he took a list of a dozen or so house descriptions with him, just in case someone in city hall was on the take. Paranoia reigned.

One late Saturday night, Dave "Skippy" Saunderson and I were on duty in his new 1965 white Mustang, just cruising around town to see where the action was. We used our own cars on duty in this special squad and the extra money for mileage helped. Late-night illegal card games, as well as the local drug dealers, were of particular interest to us on weekends. We normally worked from about nine p.m. until four a.m. or until the street died down. This night we took along a portable police radio. Unlike the small handheld portables of today, this thing was half the size of a cinder block with a thirty-inch antenna poking through the opened passenger window to get reception.

That night a call came across the radio that a fight was going down in Assunta Hall, an Italian-American club in the East End. We were only a half-mile away, so Skippy and I jumped on it. While we were certainly within our rights as police officers to respond to such calls, we had an ulterior motive. We wanted to check out the interior of Assunta Hall for future reference and identify some of those present. We'd heard rumors of illegal gambling going on in the hall, so all it took was a knowing look between us to whip the Mustang around and go for it.

We were the first officers to arrive, and from the street we could hear women screaming. Both men and women, some bloodied, were streaming down the interior staircase as Skippy and I elbowed our way up the two flights. It was pandemonium. Finally reaching the main hall and center of the disturbance, we found at least twenty people still going at it. Skippy got right to it by trying to separate two amateur pugilists.

Meanwhile, I saw the bartender bring out an oversized nightstick from beneath the bar. I went over to him and said, "Police! Gimme that goddamn stick!" He paused, gave me a puzzled look, and handed it over reluctantly. I took it and slammed it down as hard as I could flat across the bar. It sounded like a shotgun going off. Everyone in the room froze, and I said in as loud and authoritative voice as this twenty-five year old could muster, "Police. It's over! Knock it off now!" I could read this collective thought: "Police? No uniform. Just who the hell is this kid?" But it was the pause that did the trick. In truth, once any fight breaks out, all parties involved are happy to see it end. Hey, you could get hurt! The exploding nightstick did the trick and took it all down a notch. Later, Skippy joked, "Why did you do that? I had everything under control." Sure, Skippy.

HELP FROM THE FEDS?

Our unit's filing cabinets began to grow with lots of intelligence on the mobster gambling goings-on in and around Plainfield. Our work was so respected that Lieutenant Hennessey was invited by a U.S. Senate committee to give testimony concerning illegal gambling in New Jersey. He showed up in D.C. with our carefully drafted four-foot-square schematic with lines drawn between people and businesses, as well as telephone numbers and registered vehicles. It was a kind of show-and-tell of the various organized crime contacts and associations we had meticulously documented in our day-to-day observations in the field throughout central New Jersey.

Hennessey came back disgusted with the feds. He said that when his testimony was over, he was accompanied back to the FBI headquarters only to see our secret schematic thrown carelessly on top of filing cabinets in a nonsecure area. "Bunch of puffed-up college kids in suits with no street experience," he said. "One of these days their arrogant incompetence will do them in."

I learned quickly that if there was no glory in a given case, the feds had no interest in it. Also, the information flow went one way. In my dealings with the FBI, I found them to be condescending and aloof when it came to cooperation with local authorities. J. Edgar Hoover's FBI still placed its image above all else.

A couple of years after Hennessey's encounter with the feds, I had my own. While at my desk in the Union County prosecutor's office, Richie Mason slammed down his phone and erupted from his cubicle yelling, "Watts, let's go. Linden P.D. has two bank robbers pinned down in a house."

Mason was like that—quick decisions and always proactive. We sped down to Linden, just a few miles from the courthouse, to find a police/robber standoff in a residential neighborhood. The police were crouched down behind their police cars, full attention directed at a small Cape Cod house.

The Linden detective on the scene brought us up to date quickly. "These two dirt bags walked into the bank bold as could be. One waved a handgun around, scaring the shit out of the tellers and customers. We got a silent bank alarm, and just as our guys pulled up, these two took off in the Plymouth on the grass over there. It was a wild ride to get here, but they are holed up in that house."

We concealed ourselves as best we could behind the cars just as two FBI agents pulled up and joined the group. Hats positioned just right, suits pressed perfectly, and arrogance in abundance, they sauntered over, standing erect and visibly unconcerned about the possibility of gunshots from the house. After a brief conversation, both the agents walked out in front of the cars and started up the sidewalk leading to the house. Mason and I exchanged exasperated glances and cautiously stood upright.

The feds walked right in the front door of the house announcing, "FBI! Give yourselves up!"

We all knew there were two bad guys with at least one handgun inside who were, given all the law enforcement surrounding them, likely pretty desperate at this point. But the feds continued their nonchalant entry into the house as if they were making a pizza delivery.

We searched the house and, at first, found no one. As cops do, we all stood around talking and trying to figure out how the cops who saw them go into the house could have screwed up. Then someone hissed, "Quiet!" The Linden detective shushed us with one hand and pointed up toward the attic with the other. He whispered, "I heard some shuffling from upstairs."

That's all those two feds needed. They located the hallway hatch to the attic, grabbed a kitchen chair, and aligned it with the two-foot-square hatch. One of the feds put his foot on the chair, as if to climb onto it when Mason said, "What the hell are you doing? You wanna get shot?"

The agent made a sour face and got up on the chair. He pulled out his revolver and, with the other hand, raised the hatch and peeked into the attic, his gun held just in front of his nose because of the cramped space. If it weren't such a dangerous act, we would have been laughing at his inexperience.

Lucky for that FBI agent, the crooks gave up without a shot fired. We were all relieved that it turned out the way it did, but all the cops and detectives present were shaken by the way the feds handled it. We were sure that young agent would get it right in the head. This was an example of federal law enforcement at its worst. Their training was limited to intellectual criminal justice programs and theory, not good old-fashioned street experience.

Years later the FBI learned the hard way when two of its agents were killed in a shootout in Miami. In April 1986, eight agents outnumbered two serial bank robbers but were outgunned and lacked field experience to take on the tough guys who had been hitting banks all along the boulevard. The agency's street tactics changed after that tragedy, and the FBI, to its credit, admitted its mistakes and lectured on that case to local agencies around the country.

WEDDING CRASHERS

One Saturday morning, Hennessey called me and said to pick him up at home and to bring my wife's Ford Falcon station wagon. "David, my boy, we are crashing a wedding!"

The boss and I went to a church in South Plainfield

and began taking down license plates of all the vehicles in the lot. Up and down each lane, our little white Falcon wagon crawled. I drove while Hennessey read the plates into a recorder. All the while, a set of venetian blinds in the attic of a nearby house kept fidgeting. Then there was a guy walking around measuring the church windows. You see, this was a mob wedding, and the feds were in the attic taking photographs and messing with the blinds. The state police undercover guys were loitering around the church windows with a tape measure. Who knows what other agencies were in the game?

Hennessey said they were all acting silly. Mob guys expect the cops to show up, so we just boldly rode up and down and took the plates. Hennessey, ever the pragmatist, refused to be caught up in the phony secret-agent mentality. Why would we be taking down the plate numbers? Well, don't you think law enforcement might be interested in who was in attendance and how we might identify them in the future?

When I showed Linda the list of plate numbers and names taken down and distributed by all the cooperating agencies, one line entry read, "1960 Ford Falcon owned by Linda R. Watts, wife of Plainfield detective." Poor Linda. Sorry, sweetie. Goes with the territory.

THE BIG APPLE

On Saturday night, November 22, 1965, Skippy and I spotted two known and convicted druggies, "Ukie"

Nelson and Corrie Heard, heading out of town toward Route 22. Believing they were on their way to score drugs, we followed in Skippy's Mustang. As it happened, this was the same night as the PBA Ball, where all the off-duty cops and the brass were dancing and drinking somewhere nice. Meanwhile, we were tailing two creeps east on Route 22.

They kept going east on Route 22, way out of our jurisdiction. We were able to see they had a young female in the car with them, and at traffic lights they would take turns changing the seating arrangement with the girl always in the backseat (use your imagination). We were sure they would stop in Newark or maybe Elizabeth to score drugs, but they didn't. This was before cell phones, of course, so there was no way to call for instructions or assistance and no time for a pay-phone stop without losing them. Instead, we just kept tagging along after them. We went through the Holland Tunnel and northbound in New York City. They made a couple of stops, apparently looking for drugs, and during one stop, we pulled over in front of a fire hydrant and waited. Up ahead I saw a uniformed beat cop peek out from the entrance of a liquor store. He then just popped back in for a few minutes and repeated his look-see up and down the street. He didn't look happy.

"Skippy, this looks like a bad neighborhood," I said. "Even the cops are afraid."

Then a green and black NYPD patrol car slowly crept up on Skippy's side. The uniformed passenger cop said, "There must be a reason for you two New Jersey white boys to be parked in front of a fire hydrant in this neighborhood."

Skippy slowly reached for his ID when we saw the business end of the passenger cop's .38 leveled at us, resting in the lower front corner of the cruiser's open window. The usually cool Skippy stammered a little this time, trying to get out what we were there for. Before slowly moving off, the NYPD guys warned us not to get out of the car. "It's not safe here, fellas!"

We were at Lexington Avenue and 116th Street in Spanish Harlem. Here we were from a relatively small city in central New Jersey where crime was nothing compared with NYC. Naïve youngsters that we were, we stuck with it and followed Nelson and Heard back to Plainfield and pulled them over just inside the city line.

Their license plates did not match the car, and Heard was driving on the revoked list, so we arrested them. We knew that both had long criminal records, so we approached with guns drawn. Even then, Nelson looked like he was debating whether to cooperate. From the front passenger seat he looked up at me, narrowed his eyes, and was clearly trying to make a decision. I cocked my head a little and gave him one of those movie lines: "Ukie, don't even think about it." He mustered a sigh of resignation and slowly got out with his hands up. We cuffed them both and radioed for backup. Later we learned the girl was only fourteen years old and pregnant. We thought for sure we would find drugs in the car, but no luck there.

When Lieutenant Hennessey got our report, he

went off the rails. "You both should know better than to leave the city under those circumstances and without anyone knowing where you were or what you were doing. What the hell were you thinking?"

He went on to read the rest of the riot act to us, then with a smirk he couldn't hide said, "Okay, get out of my office and go fight some local crime." We knew Hennessey appreciated our intentions. After all, our unit was supposed to be proactive, and that surely meant being creative. Thinking back on it, I see now that Hennessey had his hands full with us. But our squad had a "go get 'em" mandate, so we were expected to push the envelope from time to time.

Heard and Nelson were bailed out and back on the street the next day. We thought about child endangerment charges against them, but the prosecutor advised against it. They would argue this was only an innocent drive to NYC and back. It was often like that. We would put a lot of time and effort into a case, only to have the criminals bailed out and back out on the street before we had finished our paperwork.

Too Close for Comfort

Whenever Skippy and I worked together on weekend nights, we found ourselves involved in something. We were supposed to be proactive and not just wait for crimes to come to us. I recall a Saturday night on North Avenue, just across from the main railroad station. It was two a.m. and relatively quiet. I parked and we got out and took a walk along the railroad embankment to get a better idea of what might be going on. We could see lights on in an apartment on the fourth floor of a tenement across North Avenue and hear the deep tones of men laughing.

Deciding to explore, we crossed the street, and Skippy jumped up and pulled down the fire-escape ladder. We climbed up the fire-escape stairs to the fourth floor, where we hid behind some bed sheets that were hanging to dry, our lower legs barely visible. On the other side of the closed window we could see an illegal card game in process. The problem was, we didn't have a search warrant and were in no position to claim this was taking place in plain sight. After all, we weren't just walking by; we climbed a ladder and four floors to get there. Anyway, there were far too many players for the two of us to tangle with. Then the unthinkable happened.

The window opened and a large black man stepped out onto the fire escape with us. Just a couple of feet away, and on the other side of the sheets, he decided to relieve himself over the edge of the fire escape. I looked over at Skippy and shook my head. Skippy in those days was capable of doing anything before thinking it out first. Just a foot or so away from us, the guy then zipped up and went back in through the window, none the wiser. We made a quiet and hasty retreat down the fire escape and filed our report the next day. We thought we had located the "big game" in Plainfield. Maybe we did, but it turns out it moved from week to week. We had stumbled upon it, but could do nothing about it.

Making It Up As We Go

I was usually teamed with either Skippy or Fred Stranzenbach. If ever two people were opposites, it was Skippy and Fred. Ever the attention-getter, Skippy was named for his hyped-up nature. His puffed-up wise-guy attitude belied his thin physique, and his mouth was his biggest enemy. He once walked up to a young black driver who had just peeled rubber at an intersection and said, "What's the action with the traction, Jackson?"

No one could say, however, that he wasn't a good cop. He had plenty of attitude, but you couldn't help appreciating his courage. He was creative, as well. For example, we were trying to follow a particularly slick old numbers runner with no success. The guy had a defense method all his own. He drove so slowly that if you tried to follow him, you would be falling all over yourself. Skippy came up with a plan, though. He dressed the part and got on his ten-speed bike, logging the numbers runner's whole route from that vantage point. When it came time to take him down, Skippy came up with another ruse, but he had to sell it first. "He will never suspect we are from this unit if we uniform up and check out a marked radio car," he argued. "We'll just pull him over like a traffic stop. Then we'll hit him with the search warrant." We were well known to the local gamblers and junkies, so we did anything we could do to conceal our identities, even if it meant looking like regular uniformed cops to get the job done.

Some gamblers had a hole in their car floorboard and would dump "their work" through the hole if they spotted us coming in their direction. The paperwork would be prefolded with an elastic band around it, making it the size of a walnut. Until we caught on to that one, our search would turn up nothing, as the evidence was likely lost amid other road litter a hundred yards back. Skippy's idea worked well. That was one surprised numbers runner when I pulled the search warrant out of my uniform coat at his driver's door.

Quiet, Quirky, but Always on the Job

Fred Stranzenbach, on the other hand, was quiet and quirky. He was fearless and earned the nickname "Crazy Strazzbach." That's just what Fred wanted.

He didn't always get his English right. He would say, "Hey, Watts, are ya beinhave?" Fred had some really strong opinions, but he was all cop, too, and I mean all the time.

Years earlier when in uniform, Fred took a bad beating on Plainfield Avenue and was found lying in the gutter, his gun belt hanging from a telephone pole. He was left with a bad set of false teeth from that incident. Fred spotted the guy weeks later and arrested him.

Fred was the quintessential prowler. He didn't talk much in the car and was in a constant state of readiness. He had an uncanny ability to spot something out of place. Once on uniformed patrol with Fred, we were slowly cruising east on South Avenue when he suddenly said, "Get that car ahead of us. They just broke into the cash machine in the laundromat we just passed." Fred put all that together in seconds, and we had ourselves a good bust. I pulled over the car and two out-of-towners had about twenty pounds of quarters, nickels, and dimes scattered over the backseat and floor.

Working in the company of these ex-military, hard-drinking tough guys, you couldn't stay naïve for long. For all our personal foibles, the members of this small, special squad worked well together.

While it was tough trying to put a tail on the bad guys who were watching for us, years later, as a private investigator, it was a lot easier to follow insurance claimants or the corporate bunch. They didn't have a clue. But on the job in Plainfield, we constantly had to come up with new ideas—like the time Freddie and I reported to Hennessey's office one summer day and were told we were going to make a movie.

Smile, You're On Candid Camera!

The intersection of Plainfield Avenue and West Fourth Street was the epicenter of illegal gambling in Plainfield's African American community. With lookouts everywhere, it was impossible to conduct surveillance anywhere within sight of that intersection without being discovered. Dan Hennessey came up with an idea to overcome that problem.

The lieutenant wanted us to hide in the back of the city's traffic-light repair truck, parked within easy camera distance of the intersection. The traffic-light guys were brought into our scheme and parked us every day in just the right spot, then drove off in another truck to do their work. No one on the street would suspect the police to be stashed in the truck that was fixing traffic lights in the neighborhood all the time.

We cobbled together a little coop in the back of the truck consisting of a couple of old wooden milk crates and a tarp along with a ton of tools, ropes, and other nondescript junk. We spent the better part of the summer of 1965 on our stomachs, sweltering in the back of that truck. It was worth it. We shot more than two thousand feet of Super 8-millimeter film and documented an ongoing illegal lottery operation. We zoomed in on license plates and individuals as they made their daily deliveries of the numbers slips and money to the "bank," where the tally is figured up. The money and slips go out of town to the mafia mobsters who actually run and benefit the most from these operations.

Early on, we figured out their game. Cars would stop in front of the second sidewalk-level door in from West Fourth Street on Plainfield Avenue, and the same man would come out from a darkened hallway, cross the sidewalk, and receive small objects from people in cars that pulled to the curb. He then would go back in and deposit these small objects (money and numbers slips) into a mailbox attached to the wall. To the untrained eye, all this was lost in the clutter of normal activity on the street.

Every so often, a woman would come down the inner stairway, put something in the mailbox, and then go back up and out of sight. Undoubtedly, she was taking action on the phone upstairs. All this was documented clearly on film. We were able to figure out their delivery system, but only because we could remain in our little hideout long enough to see it. To the casual passerby, there wasn't anything criminal going on, but the film produced a strong suggestion that there was.

Near the end of the surveillance, we had a scare that we were able to laugh about later, but it was anything but funny at that moment. It almost blew the whole job. In order to get certain angles from within our little pile of boxes and canvas, we had to scrunch forward on our bellies and get our faces close to the small opening in the slats. Suddenly one day Freddie pulled back and hissed, "Shit, we're made. That guy right there looked right at me . . . eyeball to eyeball." Evidently, when we were back a few inches operating the camera or using binoculars in a straight line, we could not be seen; but when we pushed a little forward to get that better angle, the daylight coming in illuminated our faces enough to be spotted, but only if the other guy was near the truck in the right position on the sidewalk at the same time. Timing is everything in life, and this time it couldn't have been worse.

Whispering within our little hothouse, we agreed to do nothing and stay put. We watched as "Mr. Eyeball" scurried back to the corner about four hundred feet away and reported what he saw. His frantic gestures in our direction left no doubt about the topic of conversation.

A short time later the corner group came up with a plan. They sent a blind man up the street guided by a little girl and placed him right next to the truck. Apparently, their theory was that the blind have exceptional hearing and he would be able to confirm Mr. Eyeball's story. The blind man stayed there for a good hour, sometimes leaning on the truck, sometimes tapping on its side, but always listening for anything that remotely resembled, for example, two detectives under a tarp filming an illegal numbers operation.

Finally, and much to our relief, he cane-tapped off, mumbling, "Ain't nobody breathin' in that truck, for sure!" He was almost right, because we held our breath most of that time. When he left, we could relax our aching muscles a bit. The corner group teased Mr. Eyeball the rest of the day and went about its business of running numbers on the corner. We restarted our filming, as well.

Finally, it came time to scoop up the Plainfield and Fourth Street gamblers. Our intent was to grab as many as possible with the numbers slips on them, then charge the others with conspiracy based on the associations we captured on film.

Hennessey put me back under the tarp in the traffic-light truck alone, but with a two-way radio. I was to let the other detectives know what was happening. We let the action go on for several hours, and when it seemed there should be enough evidence in the mailbox and in the pockets of those involved, I was to signal our guys to move in.

We used two vans with cops in the back parked several blocks away. Hennessey drove one van, and Fred the other, both in disguise. Fred wore a floppy hat and dark-rimmed glasses, and Hennessey wore a raincoat and a woman's wig. It all added a certain panache to the exercise.

On my signal, one at a time the vans swooped down and caught the suspects crossing the intersection on foot. The timing was such that as the van hesitated momentarily almost mid-intersection before turning left, the side doors swung open and the player was snatched right off his feet and into the van by Skippy and two of the other detectives. They did it so fast that it took a long time for the corner bunch to catch on. As the van headed east on West Fourth Street, the discombobulated gambler was read his rights, searched, arrested, and handcuffed. The van then went around, got in line, and did it all over again. We were able to arrest several of the suspects for possession of illegal lottery slips.

Our two thousand feet of film was presented to the Union County grand jury, resulting in seventeen conspiracy indictments and almost as many for possession of illegal lottery slips. The prior-convicted gamblers got some jail time, and the others were sent back to municipal court on misdemeanor charges. The successful investigation and resulting arrests went a long way toward reinstating the reputation of the Plainfield Police after the earlier grand jury presentment scandal. What's more, that summer's work became a training film shown at police academies for years to come. During the trial, aging Judge John Barger, when he was awake enough, couldn't quite grasp what was happening on the projection screen. "All I see is a bunch of people walking around on the corner, but if we must, continue, Mr. Prosecutor."

In fact, the case got some resistance at the county where I was working by the time it went to trial. Since I knew all of the players and had taken part in the investigation, I was assigned to work with Assistant Prosecutor Leslie Glick in trial preparation and presentation. Glick was not enthusiastic about prosecuting these illegal gamblers. "This is bullshit," he told me. "You guys are picking on a bunch of small-time black gamblers and letting the big fish off the hook. But I'll do my job, even if it stinks."

"Mr. Glick," I replied, "all due respect, but it was your own grand jury that handed down that presentment against the Plainfield Police a couple of years ago. So, do you or don't you want us to address illegal gambling in Plainfield?"

There I go again, shooting my mouth off. Glick went to the prosecutor, Leo Kaplowitz, and complained about my attitude. When I was called in to Kaplowitz's office, Glick was seated in front of the prosecutor's desk with a smug look on his face.

Kaplowitz started the conversation, "David, Mr. Glick here tells me you are not satisfied with his handling of this gambling case. What do you have to say?"

In a slow and subdued manner, I responded, "Mr. Prosecutor, I only reacted to Mr. Glick's continuous stream of disparaging remarks about my former unit and his contention that we were persecuting the blacks. Sir, as I said to Mr. Glick, it was your grand jury that concluded not enough was being done to curb illegal gambling in Plainfield, and our unit was put together to address that very problem. On a personal note, my partner and I spent all of last summer under a tarpaulin in the back of a truck taking that film, and that very same grand jury came down with indictments based on that film. I feel that Mr. Glick has a different agenda here and needs to understand what our motivation was in pursuing these gambling arrests. That's what I have to say."

Mr. Kaplowitz paused a moment, then looking at Glick asked, "Can you continue with this case?"

Glick, slightly off guard, said he could. Kaplowitz asked me if I could work with Glick on the case, to which I nodded my head. That was it. Kaplowitz quietly said, "Get back to work, and no more of this."

For me, this was a victory. Glick knew he overplayed his hand. He didn't expect the kid would speak up as he did. He thought, as a fellow lawyer, he could convince Kaplowitz to reprimand me, or worse, downgrade the case and maybe have it dismissed. We worked together at trial, but Glick handled the plea bargains himself. Defense counsel Norm Abrams must have been happy at the concessions Glick made during those talks, because most of the first-time defendants got off with a small fine and no jail time. Nevertheless, I was proud of that job and our unit.

Just in case you were wondering whatever happened to Howard Swint (the guy we watched in the green Pontiac back on Rushmore Avenue), he was among those known and convicted gamblers scooped up that day and he did some jail time. I imagine that "Mr. Eyeball" earned a name upgrade to "Mr. I Told You So!"

You might also ask whatever happened to those two bad sergeants from the grand jury presentment. They were both taken out of the detective bureau and reassigned to uniform patrol. While not quite a demotion, it was quite a comeuppance. There was not enough evidence to charge, dismiss, or demote them, but they were stigmatized for the rest of their careers. Both eventually retired. One went on to a security supervisor job with AT&T. The other sold real estate.

Fritz! Fritz! Fritz!

We had been doing some surveillance in the East End of Plainfield, and it became clear that a couple of weekends a month there was a big late-night game going on at the Carmine Tino residence on East Sixth Street. Cars were parked all over the place, some of which were owned by *known and convicted gamblers* (those magic words for a search warrant). Hennessey got the warrant and we got the call at home to meet in the parking lot of a local school to receive further instructions. We knew this meant a raid, but no specifics would be handed out until the last minute.

Some of the more trusted uniformed guys were told to show up in civilian clothes. We followed Hennessey's plan to a T, but the plan was put together in daylight and carried out at night. Half of us were to approach from the street and the other half from the rear, which meant crossing neighboring yards on the next street over. It was a fiasco. First, all the dogs in the neighborhood sounded off. Then portly George Beck, a really good guy but not what you would call the athletic type, had trouble getting over a backyard fence. When he finally made it with a hefty push from someone in the rear, he landed on a ten-foot-long piece of corrugated aluminum roofing. It sounded like a drum roll, reverberating in the night air. The dogs got louder. Then came an air compressor-like "Shhhhhh!" from the rest of the backyard crew. So much for surprise.

They weren't faring any better at the front of the house. We had decided that the best way into this old, two-and-a-half-story residence was to trick someone into opening the heavy oak front door. Larry Watson, the only African-American in the detective bureau, was appointed to ring the doorbell. I suppose he was chosen because he was the least known as a cop and had a young, innocent-looking face. Mrs. Tino came to the door and peaked between the curtains, but didn't open it. Watson asked for Mr. Tino and she walked back down the hall calling for her husband. With his nose to the window in the door and seeing that the ruse wasn't going to work, Watson spit out of the side of his mouth, "Fritz! Fritz! Fritz!"

The several raiders closest, hidden in the shrubs around the porch, were puzzled. "What did he say? Fritz . . . what the hell is fritz?" To Larry, of course, fritz meant "no good" or "the fritz is on." No one in the immediate vicinity got it, but Detective Richard Mason, farther back in the driveway, did get it, and he acted. Oh, did he act! Richie Mason is a big guy, and when he came up onto the porch under a full head of steam, he lifted tall, skinny Larry Watson off his feet and both went crashing right through that solid oak door—glass shards, broken framework, Watson, Mason, and all.

That crash, though not part of the plan, gave the rest of us in the back of the house the signal that the show was on. Never wanting to be left out of the action, cops went pouring into the home wherever they could find an opening. Some bashed in the cellar windows where the bulk of the gaming was going on, and others, including yours truly, went through a side door and onto a landing leading up into the kitchen and down into the cellar area. After all the excitement and pent-up energy leading up to this moment, the adrenaline was pumping and we were ready to get the bad guys.

I started down the steps with a crowbar in my hand amid screams coming from the women upstairs and the deeper-voiced, "What the fuck!" coming from the players in the basement. Right then, an Italian-looking man in his forties, and in fairly good shape, slowly came up the stairs toward me. He had a Tony Curtis curl on his forehead, his collar was turned up, and his shirt was open showing a lot of dark black chest hair supporting gold chains. A cigarette dangled from his lips. He calmly confronted me with that almost painful Dean Martin expression—one eyebrow painfully scrunched down and the other up, looking like he was about to break into song: "Everybody loves somebody, sometime . . ." I gripped the crowbar tighter, but he said in the coolest of tones, "Sonny, are you going to hit me with that thing?" I guess I looked like I might do just that. After a pause of a second or two, we both laughed uneasily. He turned around and joined his gambling colleagues, now lined up near a pool table that had been converted into a craps table. The cellar looked like a miniature casino complete with card tables, a roulette wheel, and lots of cash everywhere.

Upstairs, the guys were rounding up a few other card players. Once things calmed down, Hennessey asked, "Where is Serrido?" We knew him as "Halfie" Serrido, named for his slight build, one of those "known and convicted gamblers" whose presence on other occasions— his car parked at the Tino house—allowed Lieutenant Hennessey to get the search warrant in the first place. We turned the place inside out, but no Halfie.

Some days following the Tino arrests we learned that Serrido was indeed present during the raid, but dove under the bed in the master bedroom when the front door exploded. Whenever a searching cop entered that bedroom, he reached up and grabbed the bedsprings with fingers and toes, lifting himself up just far enough to avoid detection should the officer lean over to look under the bed. The joke was on us, but we took it in good humor. Whenever we saw Halfie on the street after that we yelled out, "Hey, Halfie, been hanging around any strange bedrooms lately?"

Later, when I worked in the Union County prosecutor's office, another gambling raid gave birth to similarly accidental humor. The raiding party was to gain entry to this three-story triangular-shaped 1930ish office building on Elizabeth Avenue by first isolating the elevator operator. The plan was to get off at the second floor and line up at the four doors along the hallway. At the signal, we were to break down the doors and rush in to execute the search warrant on this sports-betting parlor. I was, of course, partnered with Richie Mason, and when the signal was given, Richie and I slammed into the door. It didn't give. We hit it again, harder this time. I can still see the look on the guy's face seated at the desk inside taking telephone action. The interior of that office had been paneled right over all the doors, except one. That poor guy heard a crash, and the next thing he saw was two guys with guns out, coming right through his paneled wall.

The scene was right out of *The Godfather*. The "sport" was sitting between wall photographs of Dean Martin and Frank Sinatra. Ol' Blue Eyes was crooning away on the tape machine, though barely audible above our excited ruckus. The poor guy tried to get rid of the evidence by throwing it out the window, but Captain Steve McGlynn was down on the street catching the fluttering evidence as it drifted down. We arrested four that day.

On another gambling raid in Elizabeth, I had a scare. We knew from an informant that the bets were being taken over the phone in an attic area. The problem was getting up there in time to grab the evidence before it was destroyed. Richie Lazo and I were assigned a side door. When the signal was given, we kicked in the first door and went into the kitchen, then we rushed to another door that led to a stairway to the attic. The door was locked. All the while, we could hear other raiders having problems getting access to the building. I took a step back and kicked as hard as I could just under the door handle. The door flew open, slamming against the inside wall, just missing a small child who stood wide-eyed as we flew past him up the stairs to the attic. That was just inches from injuring a child. We all talked later about how to avoid such situations in the future. There was no simple answer.

Once in the attic, we grabbed the bookie taking bets in Spanish on the phone. I was assigned to take action on the phone with a recorder attached. The phone rang and I became the stand-in "Español" bookie for the day. My high school Spanish teacher, Mrs. Haberman, would have been proud.

Many believe that gambling is a victimless crime. We would get challenged on that all the time. "What harm does a little betting do? What the heck—you could win some money and it's just fun to play. You shouldn't be locking people up for gambling." Today some form of legal gambling is present in just about every state, but the damage that gambling has on families is well documented. It is a serious addictive activity for many that takes food off the table and sends mortgage or grocery money down to the track. There are buses that take senior citizens to the casinos in Atlantic City, encouraging them to blow their social security checks on gambling. There's just something morally wrong with that.

Overall, it is the gangsters who profit by preying on this human weakness. An illegal lottery, or numbers bank as it is known, pays five hundred or six hundred to one, but your chance of winning is 999 to one. But even that's better odds than a state-run operation. Yes, there have to be winners to keep them coming back, and regular players know the odds are stacked against them, yet they play anyway. Is that rational behavior?

The bottom line is that illegal gambling finances other and more socially aberrant vices, such as illegal drugs, prostitution, and loan sharking. Business owners are particularly vulnerable. The mob is very good at moving in on a business and pulling off a "bust out," taking over the business in exchange for credit against an outstanding gambling debt. They run the business down and suck every penny they can out of it. They order inventory on the business credit accounts and keep it or sell it elsewhere, leaving the storeowner stuck with the bill and ultimate bankruptcy. It's that or broken legs. In *The Sopranos* television series, Tony Soprano's takeover of his friend's sporting goods store for a gambling debt is an excellent example of a "bust out."

By the way, *The Sopranos* is as close to the real life of mobsters as I have ever seen. Of course, these guys are dangerous, antisocial, and psychopathic; far be it from me to say anything sympathetic about their nature, but I can't help laughing sometimes at their thought processes. The most entertaining book I ever read about these bad boys was Jimmy Breslin's *The Gang that Couldn't Shoot Straight.* It will make you laugh out loud if you can still find a copy.

Chapter Four

Channeling Fear

No question about it, the area around Plainfield Avenue and West Fourth Street was the epicenter of Plainfield's criminal activity. Fresh out of training in May 1961, my first midnight shift was walking that beat. When I reported for that first real night on the job in my spanking-new blues, Lieutenant Ralph Mondoro greeted me as a new member on his shift.

Mondoro looked up from his paperwork when I walked in and said, "Well, Watts, I have you down for Post Six, Plainfield and Fourth. What do you think about that?"

I bravely replied, "Hey, Lieutenant, gotta do it sometime . . . might as well be tonight." Mondoro couldn't hear my churning stomach over the change-of-shift background conversation. Nobody wanted to work Post Six . . . ever. But it was like worrying about a dentist appointment. When it finally came, it wasn't that bad at all.

Mondoro, along with his dispatcher, Bill Cotter,

both had metal plates in their heads, the result of a bad police car accident. Years before, the two partners were on their way to a house fire with the patrol car siren blaring. They collided with a city fire truck, its siren screaming as well, so neither driver could hear the other. A fireman hanging on the side of the truck was killed when he was thrown off and flew through Mulford Insurance Agency's front plate glass window. After that, both the police and firemen took special care at intersections. Emergency responses were controlled—no cowboy driving allowed.

Lieutenant Mondoro and I always got along well. He was very deliberate and in control. Nobody dared cross him, however. He could cut you off at the knees with a look. My first night on Post Six was memorable in that I arrested a loiterer who refused to "Move along!" I was being tested by the street, as well as by Mondoro. When I came in with my man, I caught his half-smile when he took out the booking card.

My favorite recollection of Lieutenant Mondoro took place during the Plainfield riot in the tumultuous summer of 1967. All the major news outlets were gathering in front of headquarters, including the highly recognizable Gabe Pressman of WNBC-TV, NBC's flagship station. No one was being allowed into the building except police officers. Pressman, however, would have none of that. Patrolmen John Waldron and Bob Miller were bookends guarding the front door, but Pressman persisted. Finally, not one to be intimidated by the more than five hundred collective pounds of these two officers, Pressman tried pushing his way past them. Waldron and Miller each grabbed an elbow and arrested Pressman on the spot.

"You want to go in that badly?" Waldron asked. "Okay, buddy, you are under arrest." The two officers literally carried him into the building and up to Lieutenant Mondoro at the booking window.

They walked right past me, and I can attest that Pressman's feet never once hit the floor amidst a flurry of sputtering protestations, "Do you know who I am? I'll have your job . . ."

On the other side of the booking window, Lieutenant Mondoro calmly approached with booking card poised. He inserted the card into the top of the typewriter, ceremoniously twirled the carriage with both hands, then looked Pressman directly in the eye and said, "Name?"

Pressman glanced up at Waldron and Miller on either side, then back at Mondoro. After a pause of several seconds, Pressman realized his situation and visibly deflated.

He responded, "Pressman, Gabe." To which Mondoro asked, "Is that with one or two S's?"

Pressman nearly lost his job over that incident. Months later a deal was worked out, but Pressman, the arrogant New York hotshot, was certainly brought down a few pegs by our officers on that day. It also came at a time when we needed a little psychological boost. More on the Plainfield riot later.

MR. COOL

Freddie Stranzenbach and I helped out the regular detectives by cruising around town looking for anyone with an active arrest warrant, often on Saturdays. Freddie knew a lot of the criminal element there, having arrested many of them over the years. Besides, there was always the chance one of them would be carrying numbers or drugs, and the arrest warrant was a great excuse to search them—all quite legal, by the way.

One day we were driving down Plainfield Avenue and Freddie pulled to the curb. "Let's check this guy out. Ain't seen him around here before."

In the sixties an officer didn't need a reason to question someone. You just walked up and demanded ID and threw out some pointed questions. The subject in Freddie's sights was a tall, slim, muscular black man in his late twenties. He wore a black leather jacket and matching beret. The thin moustache, polished fingernails, and gold chains just oozed "cool." He was new in town, and Freddie always kept up with "the traffic." Mr. Cool was respectful and answered our questions without an attitude. He spoke softly and deliberately, his relaxed posture holding up the storefront. After we drove on, Freddie said, "Something about that guy . . . I don't know. We'll keep an eye on him."

A month later I was yanked out of dreamland by a three a.m. phone call. Lieutenant Hennessey said, "Don't ask any questions. Just get up and meet us at four thirty at

Cook School." I had calls like this before and knew it was a police raid. It's always done with a last-minute call to prevent an innocent slip or, worse, someone intentionally tipping off the bad guys.

When I pulled into the school parking lot, there were at least fifty cars from a dozen different police agencies parked all over the back lot. I knew this would be something big. Inside I grabbed a coffee and a donut (of course) then found Freddie. Before receiving our arrest packet, we walked around the school gym greeting some of our cops and those from nearby towns, the county sheriff, and state police.

The shocker came when I looked across the gym floor. There, holding up the front of the stage, was Mr. Cool, the same guy we dressed down on Plainfield Avenue the month before. Same leather jacket, same beret, even the same nonchalant pose. He smiled, walked over, and introduced himself as Leon Adams, a New Jersey State Trooper undercover narcotics detective. He actually thanked us for rousting him that day. "It gave me some street cred. You guys have no idea how well respected you are out there, but you knew I wasn't right, didn't ya?" Nodding his head in a knowing way, he added, "It's a good thing for me that you were the only ones." Adams had been buying illegal drugs for two months and the time had come to make arrests.

That raid was something else. The combined force arrested more than twenty and seized heroin and marijuana by the pound. Cocaine, crack, crank, and the designer drugs were not yet on the scene in the sixties, at least not in this community. Our guys also came up with knives, a shotgun, pistols, and even a machine gun. When the door went down, a drug dealer was diving for the machine gun in the closet, but someone tackled him first. The piece was loaded and ready to go. At another house Sergeant Bernie McColgan dodged a bowling ball thrown down the stairs at him; but, all in all, most arrestees were caught in their beds and gave up without a fight. Thankfully, there were no guns fired or injuries on either side. That is the mark of excellent planning and execution. Today, fifty years later, drug raids are conducted in the same way.

Going the Distance for Your Partner

Fred Stranzenbach and I were out again trying to serve warrants. We were talking to a group of young black kids on Plainfield Avenue when Fred said, "There's Curtis Bates. He's a gambler and a wise guy."

Freddie was always right about stuff like that, so we approached Bates, who was in his early forties, six feet four, about 230 pounds with not an ounce of fat. His head was shaved and he had nasty eyes. Freddie told him he should move along. "No loitering, Curtis." Admittedly, Freddie had that Germanic arrogant air about him and it set Bates off. Words flew, and Bates took a swing at Fred. He missed, but then grabbed Fred by his lapels and jerked him upward, almost off the ground. I guess Bates wasn't too concerned about skinny old me at 175 pounds and just six feet, but he underestimated the bond between partners. The code is we make this arrest or go down together.

Instead of taking Bates head on with Fred, I stepped behind him, jumped up, and got him around the throat between my right forearm and bicep. I thought I might pull him backward away from Fred and walk him over to the car. Instead, I found myself in midair, dangling off the back of this immovable hulk. He released Fred, which meant he could twist around and turn on me at any second. Realizing this, my leverage lessons from judo classes kicked in. I pushed my right hip into Bates's back and leaned over to my left in such a way that bent him back farther, causing a lot of pressure on his throat and neck. I dared not let him go. I thought, *If this guy gets loose, he'll kill us both!*

Freddie, always in control and now with both feet squarely on the sidewalk, straightened his suit jacket and calmly said, "Curtis, go quietly now and I will call off my partner, who is gonna kick the shit out of your sorry ass if you don't."

Meanwhile, I was hanging on for dear life. I shot a frantic look at Fred that said, "Crazy Strazzbach, you got me into this. Why the hell are you antagonizing this monster further?" Bates, eyes now bulging and unable to speak, let alone breathe by this time, managed a head nod toward Fred and went quietly all the way to police headquarters in the backseat with me, the bad-ass skinny detective sitting next to him.

Freddie never thanked me for pulling Bates off of him, and I never expected it. It was normal business to look after your partner. The incident did, however, demonstrate to my fellow detectives that I would go the distance if called upon. That is important in the law-enforcement community. Partners have to know they can count on one another, no matter what.

CHAPTER FIVE

Narcotics: A Dirty Business

There was a story that circulated in the Plainfield Police Department for a while that illustrates just what a dirty business narcotics could be. While I was not a part of this one, I would bet it happened. Fred Stranzenbach and Lieutenant Hennessey busted a small-time drug dealer I'll refer to as Noel O. They decided to use Noel to buy drugs from bigger dealers, thus allowing our unit to work its way up the food chain to those who brought the junk into town. But Noel, code name "Mr. Christmas," would have none of it, so Hennessey and Freddie grabbed him and took him for a ride.

The story goes they took him to Hillside Cemetery at midnight to a newly dug grave. They pushed his face down into the dark, open pit and advised that he should be more afraid of them than the drug dealers. Noel worked for us for about six months before skipping town, never to be heard from again. He helped us arrest a few dealers, but never delivered the big one. I have no proof the first part of this story ever happened, but it endured by virtue of repeated telling. I will admit that some of the tactics employed were unorthodox, but you have to fight fire with fire, and the drug scene was running rampant in Plainfield at the time. After all, it was the sixties.

Regardless of whether the specifics of that story were accurate, the truth is that being a "narc" was and is a dirty business. The way to fight the drug problem is to get at the dealers, and the most direct avenue to them is through the users, who are vulnerable because of their ever-increasing need for the drug. Ergo, we catch the buyer illegally possessing the drug and leverage him or her into informing on the sellers. Putting pressure on the addicted who face serious jail time is very motivational.

Little Janie M. was a perfect example of a user put on the spot. When Richie Mason and I caught Janie with marijuana in her pocketbook on Front Street, she cried almost to the point of collapse. She was pitiful, no doubt, but here was an opportunity to get an informant into the Cross Keys Hotel and Lounge in Rahway, a nightclub rampant with illegal drug activity at that time. Richie and I spent many a weekend night in the joint trying to make buys, but the group was too smart to deal with anyone they didn't know. We told Janie that we would put in a word to the judge if she would help us. The plan was for skinny little Janie to apply for a job as a go-go dancer in the club, thus working her way into the center of the drug activity. So, Janie went to Cross Keys and told the manager of the club she wanted to have an audition.

Two days later we arranged to meet Janie behind a row of stores in Plainfield. She showed up with her right arm in a cast. "The bastards made me audition on a table," she sobbed. "I was still high from the night before, so when I got up on the table I thought I was a hundred feet in the air. I fell off and broke my arm. Please don't send me to jail!" Richie and I knew that dealing with the users like Janie had its moments, and this was just another failed attempt to get to the drug dealers. We gave her a break but looked for the next time we could call on her to get into a dealer's inner circle.

THE POLITICS OF NARCOTICS

Fred Stranzenbach and I were sent to Federal Bureau of Narcotics (FBN) School in New York City. The Drug Enforcement Agency (DEA) had not yet been formed in 1965, and the FBN was the only federal agency working on narcotic trafficking. We learned from some of the smartest and slickest characters on earth. They all had worked undercover buying drugs and setting up stings all over the country and around the world. Their war stories warranted a TV series, for sure.

When we returned to duty, we were armed with the latest methods and enhanced knowledge of how to do our jobs. We also began testifying as expert witnesses in narcotics cases. Local defense counsel could not argue with our growing experience and knowledge.

Heroin was the serious illegal drug at the time.

Today it is making a comeback, only in a much more potent and lethal form.

How do we fight this battle? Nancy Reagan's answer was "Just say no." That makes a fine poster and brings public attention to the problem, but little else. The real answer lies in attacking it at its source. Criminals in the Middle East and Far East grow the poppies that are cooked down into a morphine base and converted to heroin before shipment to the U.S. If we know that, why hasn't the drug problem been conquered years ago?

Politics. Yes, it's politics. We have international relations with certain countries, groups, and even tribes within those countries. The U.S. State Department at times may deem it expedient and necessary to overlook certain transgressions by these entities, as long as commerce flows, treaties are honored, oil is delivered, and accommodations are made for our military bases. (For more on this topic, read *The Underground Empire . . . Where Crime and Governments Embrace*, by James Mills. This 1,165-page Doubleday & Company book was published in 1986, and the scandals it describes continue today.)

We are fighting the Taliban in Afghanistan while the main source of revenue for its countrymen is growing opium poppies. Do we go after the growers to prevent American kids from getting hooked? No, it might upset our State Department's backroom dealings with those who are literally killing Americans at home. That is a major source of the illegal drugs, yet we seem helpless to do anything about it. Politics.

CHAPTER SIX

Moving on Up—Really?

One night I was at a murder scene in the East End of Plainfield when an opportunity presented itself. Mr. Caruso, a local tailor, was found sitting upright in a chair in his modest home, but quite dead, his chin resting on his chest. Two young burglars broke in, and when Caruso discovered them, they beat him to death, leaving him balanced on a dining room chair.

Not so surprising, when a case breaks that might bring notoriety, the county prosecutor would usually show up. So, as expected, Union County Prosecutor Leo Kaplowitz arrived and did the required kibitzing with the brass at the scene. Since Richie Mason, formerly a Plainfield detective, was now a detective in the prosecutor's office, I thought this situation presented an opportunity to do the same. It was time for Linda and me to get out of Plainfield. If I got a job with the county, we could live in Berkeley Heights, New Providence, or Summit—in our eyes, an improvement over Plainfield. At an opportune moment, I broached the subject with Kaplowitz. He was very gracious, saying, "Any time I can hire a Plainfield detective, I will." He invited me to come to his office in Elizabeth. For me, it was another of those "seize the moment" opportunities.

Shortly thereafter, I gave my notice at Plainfield and embarked on a new adventure at the Union County Prosecutor's Office. It wasn't easy to walk away from Plainfield where I started out, but my wife and I were more than ready to get out of Plainfield and start making a life for ourselves. I did, however, feel a kinship with many of those Plainfield cops who stayed. Some got promoted, some quit, and some quietly retired. Over the next decade, four would be killed on duty, two of whom I knew and had worked with: John Gleason and Frank Buczek. I was proud to have been in that special squad, even though it was for just two years. In retrospect, I did the right thing and never regretted it. Whenever I stopped at Plainfield HQ years later as a private investigator digging for information on someone, I was never refused. The bond was permanent.

An irritating political side note: Kaplowitz had already hired me, but because of the reality of politics, he told me to go see John Kinneally at Rahway City Hall. Kinneally was the Union County Democratic chairman and Kaplowitz was trying to score points with him. I was to register as a Democrat, then ask Kinneally to recommend me to Kaplowitz, even though I was already hired. I wanted the job, so I played the game.

Who Said That?

One of my first assignments in the Union County Prosecutor's Office was to serve as backup to Assistant Prosecutor Mike Diamond in preparation of a murder case for trial.

Paul Gordon Cary was charged with murdering a young woman by stabbing her multiple times with a large knife in the kitchen of her home in Plainfield. One of the elements of the prosecution's case was positively identifying the adult male who called the police dispatcher reporting that the victim was injured and needed help. Of course, the call was recorded and preserved as evidence. Given the timeline, only the remorseful killer or another adult male at the scene could have made that call. Other trace evidence also pointed to Cary, but proving he made that phone call would go a long way toward making the prosecutor's case. It didn't help that the first officer to arrive at the murder scene picked up the phone in that house to call it in to headquarters, thus ruining any fingerprints that might identify the first caller who obviously used that phone.

A new science had been developing since the 1940s at Bell Laboratories in Murray Hill, New Jersey, using spectrographic analysis of voice and speech patterns that supposedly could match a person's voice recording to a prerecorded sample. The technique was called voiceprint identification and, if accepted by the New Jersey courts, would bring further evidence to bear against our defendant in this case. Since this was new science, a "Frye Hearing" was ordered by Judge John Barger. Basically, that means the judge would determine if our expert witness should be allowed to testify in front of the jury in consideration of this new type of proposed evidence.

Diamond and I met with Lawrence Kersta, our expert witness, at his laboratory in Somerville, New Jersey. An electronics engineer and former employee of Bell Labs, Kersta demonstrated his amazing voiceprint machine. We were enthusiastic about our chances, but Kersta thought it would be an uphill battle, because Dr. Peter Ladefoged had been engaged by the defense. Ladefoged, an associate professor of phonetics at the University of California, Los Angeles, had testified persuasively against the scientific reliability of voiceprints in other cases. In fact, these two experts had met in the courtroom before, so the battle lines were drawn. Kersta's voiceprint identification innovation had gained some support in judicial tribunals and was accepted when he qualified as an expert in spectrographic speech analysis in a White Plains, New York, case. He gave expert testimony in a U.S. Air Force court martial, as well.

Nevertheless, Ladefoged testified in the Cary case that positive voice identification was neither scientifically accepted nor adequately tested at that time. Judge Barger ruled that Kersta's testimony would not be admitted based upon " . . . the failure of the prosecution to show general scientific acceptance of the process at this time." The judge admitted that he was impressed with Kersta and his courtroom demonstration of voiceprint analysis and believed that in the future it would be scientifically accepted. But Judge Barger was not ready to break new ground.

Cary was convicted on other evidence. Voiceprint would have its day, but not that day. Over time, Kersta and voiceprint analysis were vindicated, and most states now accept its scientific value, in measure. Even Ladefoged softened his resistance as time went by and admitted voiceprint has it place, though limited, in the courts. For years, however, these two expert combatants jousted in many other courtroom dramas around the country.

Kersta's contribution to the judicial system is immeasurable. His testimony and his voiceprint identification project convicted some and exonerated others. In time, spectrographic voice analysis became accepted science around the world, even in the venerable halls of the FBI. Today it is applied in terrorist identification among other cases.

Kersta went on to form the International Association of Voice Identification and was a respected scientific innovator up until his death at the age of eighty-six in 1994. That same year, attorney Michael K. Diamond, my boss on that case, was appointed judge of the Superior Court of New Jersey after a distinguished career in private practice. He has since retired and is affiliated with the Mandelbaum Salsburg law firm in West Orange, New Jersey. Peter Ladefoged died suddenly on January 24, 2006, at the age of eighty in London while changing planes on his way home from fieldwork in India.

It was a privilege to have been there at the beginning of voice identification's long journey toward scientific acceptance in the courts. This is a perfect example of the persistent advancement of science in conjunction with the evolution of our judicial system. In time, the courts do catch up to the science, but with due caution.

The Cary case was my first experience with expert witnesses, and it was an awakening. Since then, in my role as a legal investigator, I have located and vetted expert witnesses, as well as refuted their anticipated testimony by pointing out their own conflicting past depositions and trial testimony for my attorney clients. The most fascinating aspect of the "battle of the experts" is watching two brilliant, educated, and dedicated scientists faced with the same set of facts arrive at diametrically opposing opinions. It is truly an intellectual duel worth watching.

CHAPTER SEVEN

Riot!

For two more years I worked gambling, narcotics, and vice with Richie Mason at the Union County Prosecutor's Office. Richie was a study in contradictions. Big, bold, brash, profane, and arrogantly confident, he was also a devout churchgoing Catholic and completely corruption free. The son of a retired NYPD precinct captain, Richie had law enforcement careening through his veins. In fact, everything about Richie careened. He didn't just enter a room, he bowled it over. Richie walked leaning forward, almost breaking into a trot, wherever he went. The epitome of confidence, Richie made things happen. I played Crocker to his Kojak, just as I did back in Plainfield with Freddie Stranzenbach and Dan Hennessey.

I didn't mind being junior man again because I was learning from a good guy, though he could be overbearing at times. That was okay because he knew it. Working with Richie was like riding out a hurricane: never a dull moment.

In the summer of 1967, the U.S. Open came to

Baltusrol Country Club in Springfield, New Jersey. Our prosecutor's office was invited to participate in the security for the major golfers. Richie and I, as luck would have it, drew "The Golden Bear," Jack Nicklaus. We closely guarded Nicklaus throughout the tournament.

It was early in his career, but Nicklaus scored a stunning victory, leading all the way. I have never been one for getting autographs, but I got them all at the U.S. Open in 1967: Ben Hogan, Chi-Chi Rodriguez, Julius Boros, Gary Player, and, of course, Arnold Palmer. After all, I was only twenty-seven and still impressionable. The clubhouse food was great, too.

That year wasn't all fun and games. Just one month after the U.S. Open, all hell broke loose in Newark and then Plainfield. Our office was called in, and Richie and I found ourselves back in our hometown during the infamous Plainfield riot.

There had been unrest over a hot July weekend. It started with about four hundred young black people breaking into splinter groups, some of whom went on a destructive rampage after being evicted from one of Plainfield's city parks because they had no permit for the gathering. On Sunday at about six thirty p.m., I'd just arrived at Plainfield headquarters and was waiting for Richie when the news came over the police radio that Patrolman John Gleason had been trampled and beaten to death by an angry mob on Plainfield Avenue, the area where I had walked my first midnight tour.

I recall standing a short distance from the dispatcher's

room in headquarters when Captain Campbell's excited voice came over the ambulance radio: "Somebody call a priest and get him to the ER!" Campbell was part of the contingent of cops trying to rescue John, but it was too late. I later learned that as the responding officers and rescue squad members loaded Gleason into the ambulance, they were pelted with bricks and other debris. Bruce Tymeson, best man at our wedding and one of the three of us who started on the job together, was involved in that rescue. He said that John Gleason was beaten so badly that he was unrecognizable.

This tall, thirty-nine year-old, gentle, soft-spoken man and father of three little girls was pronounced dead on arrival at Muhlenberg Hospital. He was the first police officer to die in the line of duty in the more than eighty-year history of the Plainfield Police Department. We were all stunned. A gloom settled over the department. When the hearse carrying John passed by the front of headquarters later that week, saluting in the front row of mourners was John's father, retired police officer Lieutenant "Babe" Gleason. It was heart wrenching. Later that day in St. Mary's Church, I shared a pew with assistant prosecutor Stan Kaczarowski and fought back tears with everyone else.

Richie Mason and I stayed together and operated independently from the others during the riot. We snuck up and down the dark streets on the edge of the West End looking for those who had broken into a Middlesex, New Jersey, gun shop and stolen no fewer than forty-six

.30-caliber military carbines. At one point, the .30-caliber lead was flying all around, fired randomly by the rioters, and Richie and I ducked into the entrance to Swain's Art Store on West Front Street near Central Avenue. Richie said, "Stick with me, kid. I made it through Korea; we'll make it through Plainfield."

Meanwhile, the randomly fired ricochets were pockmarking the buildings on Front Street. Only a few of those guns were ever recovered, even though a major push was on to find them. Luckily, marksmanship was not a serious skill set of the hot heads and black militants who came in from other towns to join the battle against the "pigs" in Plainfield. The same thing took place in Newark with far more serious consequences. While Newark had twenty-six deaths, none were police officers. Plainfield lost Officer Gleason, but there were no other riot-related deaths. The Plainfield riot was shown to be the epitome of professional law-enforcement restraint.

The decent, hard-working black residents of Plainfield were petrified and stayed in their homes and out of sight. The criminal element, however, saw this as their opportunity to loot stores and commit other crimes with impunity. The Plainfield Police were joined at the scene by many other agencies, including the prosecutor and sheriff's offices, state police, and law enforcement from several neighboring towns. The New Jersey National Guard was called in—and what a sight it was when Lieutenant General James T. Cantwell and the National Guard moved in with an armored personnel carrier.

I and many others went without sleep for three days straight, but finally order was restored street by street and neighborhood by neighborhood. George Campbell, our training officer several years before and now a captain, stepped up and did the heavy lifting in terms of supervision and primary decision making in a hastily put together command post. Of course, Lieutenant Hennessey, Freddie Stranzenbach, and Skippy Saunderson, the guys in my old special squad, were in the thick of it throughout the riot. At one point, they were pinned down on top of Central Fire Headquarters with .30-caliber rounds coming out of the darkness. Hennessey led the National Guard to Bergen and West Third Streets in the armored personnel carrier to rescue several firemen in harm's way in that satellite firehouse. Lieutenant Hennessey and Captain Campbell were our heroes during the riot.

When the situation died down sufficiently, we began to rotate in and out for rest periods. I joined Linda at her mother's house in Middlesex, where she went when the whole thing broke out three days earlier. I had been without sleep for three full days and just about collapsed into bed.

In life it seems that every tragedy has its humorous side. One problem the police had during the riot was that the city streetlights illuminated the police, but not the bad guys out in the darkness. Not long into it, the police began shooting out the streetlights with their pistols. Those shots were heard all over the West End. The brass got wind of it, and over the radio came the order: "All personnel will cease and desist shooting out street lights." There was a thirty-second pause, then the .38s started popping all over again. It was the state police that ignored most of the silly orders during that first night. Good for them!

We also had a problem with moving vehicles. Police roadblocks were up everywhere, and when a car would approach, police would demand that the drivers put their lights out. Some wouldn't or didn't understand the order, and several of those cars were peppered with shotgun pellets. No one was seriously hurt, but we just didn't know the intentions of those behind the blinding oncoming lights. The police who were in vehicles not only turned out the lights when approaching a roadblock, but also made sure their riot helmets could be easily seen hanging out of the windows to avoid friendly fire. We made it up as we went along.

Nothing Like Newark

The State of New Jersey weighed in during the riot in the personages of Attorney General Arthur Sills and Paul Ylvisaker of the New Jersey Department of Community Affairs. There were also legitimate black representatives, such as brothers George and Everett Lattimore, the latter a city councilman who was to become Plainfield's first black mayor in 1981. The two brothers stepped up and mediated the release of many of the rioters in exchange for turning in guns. Most rioters were released, but just a few guns were taken out of circulation.

But also getting their fifteen-minutes of fame were young black opportunists like twenty-nine-year-old Linward Cathcart, who, according to him, represented all the "disenfranchised black youths" in the city.

On July 22, 2007, forty years after the riot in Plainfield, *The New York Times* reported on the same Linward Cathcart, now sixty-nine years of age, as he addressed several dozen people gathered at the Plainfield Quaker Meeting House. Cathcart said the 1967 riots accelerated community organizing and prompted an investigation into police brutality. Most importantly, Cathcart said that the riots helped bring black people to power in Plainfield. While Cathcart said the riots served as a step forward for the black community, he could not help lamenting what had become of the community today. "We can't honor [the riots] and be proud of this," said Cathcart, his voice rising as he denounced the poverty, drugs, and joblessness that characterize the still predominantly black West End.

Holding out a hand to the leaders of the Quaker congregation in the wooden pews, he asked them to "reach out to our community."

"We are in trouble," he said. "We need help."

Looking back over the news articles and with the benefit of nearly fifty-years of hindsight on the subject, it seems clear that Mayor George Hetfield had it right. He was quoted in the media: "There's absolutely no reason for what's happening. Our community relations in the city were very harmonious."

NEW UNIFORMS—Rookie patrolmen, Bruce Tymeson, George Sauderson and David Watts, are shown wearing the new prescribed police uniform for recruits to the Plainfield Police Department. They will wear the khaki uniforms during their training period. (Photo by Wiggins)

On the right, skinny guy with cap bill on my nose. Skippy (middle) stiking a pose, as usual and Bruce Tymeson (left) with Elvis smile. April 1961 (Photo courtesy of Courier News)

**Author taking phone bets during a gambling raid in 1966
(Author's memorabilia)**

**Author with detective
face on. Plainfield
Police Department
in 1965. (Author's
memorabilia)**

Union County Prosecutor Leo J. Kaplowitz, "Any time I can hire a Plainfield Detective, I will." I was hired on the spot at a Plainfield murder scene. (1960s internet photo)

Union County Sheriff Ralph Oriscello kicked me out of his office when I wouldn't dump a criminal case against one of his inmates. No happy face that day! (1960s photo)

Patrolman John V. Gleason murdered by a mob on July 17, 1967 (Photo courtesy of Union County Assistant Prosecutor Susan Gleason, his daughter)

Immediate scene of Gleason homicide. Under attack from a mob, he ran from corner on right and was caught beneath the railroad underpass where he was beaten to death. (Photo courtesy of Courier News)

When cars failed to stop at roadblocks, officers feared vehicular attacks, especially at night. Several had rear windows shot out like this one. (Photo courtesy of Courier News)

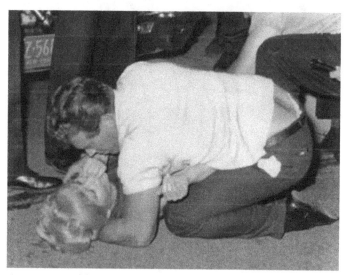

A 22 years-old Somerville, New Jersey woman is comforted by her friend after snipers opened fire on their sedan on West Fourth Street. She was hit in the leg.
(Photo courtesy of Courier News)

Plainfield, New Jersey Police Headquarters new in 1965.
(Photo couresty of Courier News)

The New Jersey National Guard arrived in Plainfield and
helped restore order. They played a large part in the search for
the stolen carbines. (Photo courtesy of Courier News)

The New Jersey State Police and The New Jersey Nation Guard
worked as a team. (Photo courtesy of Courier News)

Saint Mary's Church was overflowing with mourners.
(Photo courtesy of Courier News)

POLICE DEPARTMENT
PLAINFIELD, NEW JERSEY

TRAINING MEMORANDUM

TO: All Members of This Department
FROM: Milford S. Payne, Chief of Police
DATE: June 20, 1966
SUBJECT: The Police Department and Public Relations

The very nature of police work involves regulating and controlling the
behavior of the public, and therefore presents many unpleasant and dis-
agreeable tasks. "A policeman's lot is not a happy one."

Any discipline and control, even when used in a tactful, fair and reasonable manner, is resented by many, but when an officer acts in an
arrogant or officious manner in his endeavors to enforce any law, his
attitude is resented by all, to the detriment of the entire Police
Department. This also holds when members of the public ask us for
information or assistance.

Public relations can be employed to good advantage in convincing the
public that the police do not make the laws, but do have the responsi-
bility of enforcing them regardless of how unsound, unfair, or
unpopular the laws may seem to be. So long as a law remains on the
Statute Books, we, as police officers, are obligated to enforce it.
This fact should be brought to the attention of the public we serve
in a frank and honest manner, rather than have the police regarded as
arbitrary, overbearing and stupid for enforcing a law that may be
unpopular or seem unreasonable.

I have received several complaints recently regarding the attitude
of some members of this Department toward the general public. This
concerns me, and it should concern you. Complaints have been received
that citizens are rudely treated; profanity has been used, and in
general, conduct unbecoming a police officer has on occasion been
exhibited. This type of conduct must cease immediately.

Rudeness, failure to use common courtesy, the use of improper language
to a citizen, or any conduct by a Member of this Department, detrimental
to the Department and its responsibilities to the public, will not be
tolerated.

Let there be no double standards or display of favoritism in the enforcement of the law, if the respect of the community is desired. When a
Police Department is regarded with animosity, bitterness and resentment
by the public, it cannot hope to receive the cooperation and understanding
assistance from the community, without which there can be no truly
successful police work. A policy of "The Public Be Damned" is suicidal.

continued

POLICE DEPARTMENT
PLAINFIELD, NEW JERSEY

P.2 - The Police Department and Public Relations
      June 20, 1966

In his every-day contact with the public, a police officer should
display patience, sympathetic forbearance and understanding. It is
conceded that questions asked of him can become annoyingly repetitious
and seemingly a sign of ignorance or stupidity on the part of those
asking the questions. But it should be kept in mind that in asking
for information, direction and advice, the public is really displaying
confidence in the officer's judgment, intelligence and fund of knowledge. Any rebuffs or discourteous treatment on the part of the police
officer react unfavorably upon the department in its entirety.

Occasionally there is displayed a tendency by some police officers
to treat certain national, social, racial or religious groups with
more or less consideration than the public as a whole. It cannot be
stressed too strongly that democracy is primarily built upon the
foundation of a great many minority groups. The rights of these groups
must be carefully safe guarded or there is dangerous risk of appearing
prejudiced or discriminatory.

REMEMBER, GOOD WILL IS NOT BUILT UP OVERNIGHT, BUT IT CAN BE DESTROYED
IN THAT TIME.

Milford S. Payne
Chief of Police

mv

OFFICE OF THE COUNTY PROSECUTOR
UNION COUNTY COURT HOUSE
ELIZABETH, N. J. 07207
333-8000

LEO KAPLOWITZ
PROSECUTOR

August 1, 1967

Investigator David B. Watts
Apt. 16-B ~ 17 Farragut Road
Plainfield, N. J.

Dear Dave:

       I want to personally express to you my deepest gratitude for your assistance and the untiring efforts made by you during the Plainfield incidents.

       I know you went without sleep and often food for long periods of time, for you spent untold extra hours at the scene of activity, where your presence was most desperately needed.

       The courage displayed by you and your willingness to as sist were most gratifying to me and I want you to know that I am proud to have you as a member of my staff.

Sincerely,

LEO KAPLOWITZ
Union County Prosecutor

LK:MG

110

Barbara Mason holding bible as her husband, Richard Mason is sworn in as a prosecutor's detective in Union County in 1965. A champion squash player into his eighties, Richard is tough, smart, fearless and, above all, honest. I played "Crocker to his Kojak." (Photo from Richard Mason photo collection)

Captain George Campbell (left) and then Lieutenant Dan Hennessey about to testify at the Eastland Senate Judiciary Committee Hearings, Washington, D.C. in August, 1967. During the riot, they both stepped up and displayed the leadership we desperately needed at the time. (Photo from Hennessey Family photo collection)

Plainfield Police Captain Dan Hennessey in 1968. Several years earlier, he was author's lieutenant in the Narcotics/Gambling Plainclothes Unit. Hennessey retired from Plainfield and served another twenty years as police chief in Marple Township, Pennsylvania. (Photo from Hennessey Family photo collection)

Left to right: John Reilly, Fred Stranzenbach, and John Hicks at promotion ceremony at Plainfield City Hall in 1968. Stranzenbach and I were partners in the radio car, as well as the detective bureau. His daughter married Hicks' son and Hicks' daughter married Fred's son. (Photo from Stranzenbach and Hicks family collections)

"Clearly," the mayor added, "the Plainfield riot was an orchestrated overflow from and continuation of the Newark riot. Out-of-town agitators and militants came to the city after the first day and night of minor incidents and fanned the flames into something much larger. Officer Gleason's death on Sunday night, together with the report of the stolen carbines, ramped up the tension on both sides."

The simple fact is that Plainfield's culture was nothing like Newark's. While Newark had people living in severely neglected projects, most Plainfielders lived in one- or two-family residences. In most of these homes resided someone who was employed. They paid their taxes and most were law abiding. Sure, there were drunken fights, domestic squabbles, and fall-out from drug abuse, but nothing like inner-city Newark.

The police in Plainfield worked to improve community relations. Yes, a few officers I worked with could be labeled racist and acted on their hatred from time to time, but it was not widespread. These "bad apples" were known to all, and I and others intervened to prevent any of those guys from being overly physical during an arrest.

One incident I recall took place in the dark on South Second Street near the railroad tracks. A detective I won't identify grabbed a black vagrant and roughed him up a little. He held the poor guy by his elbows and said, "Kick his ass, Watts . . . just for fun." The vagrant was drunk and nearly incoherent. His trousers fell down and he wore no underpants. His only crime was sleeping in an abandoned car. I told that detective I had no reason to hit the guy, and if he went any further, I would report him.

The detective shouted at me, "You're not tough enough to be a cop." What he really meant was I wasn't cruel or insensitive enough. We didn't get along well after that, but he never pushed that button in front of me again. Most officers with any sense realized that we were, indeed, the thin blue line and it was far more advantageous to get along with the public than to aggravate it, no matter what your private thoughts were.

Any claims that police brutality was endemic in Plainfield were just plain wrong. There was no "us and them" attitude on the part of administration when it came to the black community. To the contrary, a great deal of sensitivity was evident coming from upstairs.

On June 20, 1966, more than a year before the Plainfield violent outbreak, Police Chief Milford S. Payne distributed a training memo to every officer. I still have this remarkable two-page missive that explicitly sets forth the public relations aspect of community policing and warns that improper behavior will not be tolerated. While I have no direct knowledge of the reason for putting out that memo, it was likely a response to bad behavior on the part of an officer such as I described earlier. That 1966 memo demonstrates the department's concerns over police/community relations and that it had a head-on approach to facing potential problems before they got out of hand.

I know that the officers with whom I worked regularly, in and out of uniform, conducted themselves properly, and if any harbored ill feelings toward African Americans, they kept it to themselves.

THE JOHN GLEASON MURDER INVESTIGATION

After the Plainfield riot and a day's rest, we were all back in Plainfield conducting the lengthy investigation of the murder of Officer John Gleason. Witnesses were interviewed and statements taken. As the inquiry went forward, we began to piece together the facts.

At the intersection of South Second Street and Plainfield Avenue, near a Central Jersey Railroad underpass, a group was looting a store. Officer Gleason, assigned to a nearby intersection, saw this taking place, so he went down to intervene. At the same time, a patrol car with two other officers responded and the crowd disbursed on their arrival, or so it seemed. The patrol car left and Gleason was about to return to his post a block away when he spotted a young black man, Bobby Lee Williams, wielding a hammer and pursuing another young black person.

Gleason tried to arrest Williams, but Williams resisted. The crowd formed again and circled around Gleason to prevent Williams's arrest. Williams, then emboldened, threatened Gleason with the hammer. This escalated to the point where Gleason fired his weapon and struck Williams several times. The mob then started in earnest after the officer, chasing him to a point under the overpass. They caught up with him, and in the melee that followed, Officer Gleason was stomped to death.

Bobby Lee Williams survived and was charged with the Gleason murder, but plead out to a lesser charge. Ultimately, arrest warrants were issued, and the job of rounding up the defendants was at hand.

On one of the arrest raids, I was assigned to one side of a house, in the driveway near defendant Wayne's (last name withheld) bedroom window. Just at dawn, I crept up to the opened window and peeked in while others were getting into their own assigned positions. Wayne was facing me, asleep and just three feet away. When the front door crashed inward, he jerked awake. I already had my gun inches from his face. Now wide-eyed, he froze, just as in the movies. The guys burst in to find Streater and me eye to eye (actually, his eye to my gun barrel). I have since wondered what it must have been like to wake up looking down the barrel of a gun.

We arrested many in that mob only to have most go free. Allegations of racism and the birth of political correctness soon washed over the investigation, and the world changed before our eyes. No doubt, state officials such as Paul Ylvisaker pulled rank on New Jersey cities in fear of further uprisings. Self-appointed black leaders like Cathcart made demands that were acceded to without question. Many of us were disgusted with our elected officials, but there was little we could do.

After an exhaustive investigation, twelve people

were indicted for the murder. Eleven were tried together. One was acquitted by order of the trial court; nine were found not guilty by the jury; and just two were convicted of John Gleason's murder. The evidence showed George Merritt struck Officer Gleason with a meat cleaver, and Gail Madden stomped on the officer and struck him repeatedly on the head with a metal shopping cart. Madden wore an orange dress, and at 250 pounds was easily identifiable by the witnesses who watched from the north side of the tracks. Both received life sentences for their actions. Merritt won several appeals. He was tried and convicted three times. His last appeal was a habeas petition in which he was granted a new trial. John Stamler, prosecutor at the time, decided not to try Merritt a fourth time . . . prosecutorial discretion. Merritt was released from state prison in 1980.

While there were dozens more mob members present when Gleason was attacked, the actions of Merritt and Madden were deemed the most egregious.

During that investigation, Lieutenant Bob Ward sent me to the offices of NBC in New York City to obtain film taken by one of their film crews. Earlier on the same day John Gleason was killed, that NBC crew drove down Plainfield Avenue with their cameras scanning the sidewalk where people were gathered. Those in charge of the murder investigation needed to know who was on the street as it related to the timing of the Gleason attack.

The people I talked to at NBC did not seem happy their film was becoming part of the murder case. I was not greeted warmly. In the end I had to push the issue. I said, "Hey, a cop was murdered. Your film might show the presence of the killers on the street at that time. Do you want it on your conscience that you refused to help?"

NBC gave over the film, but not without some dirty looks. The film did, indeed, refute statements by some that they weren't even there. It also showed many of Gleason's attackers on the street prior to the incident, which was very helpful.

Plainfield wasn't alone in its long, hot summer of 1967. In addition to Newark, riots and unrest occurred in Detroit, Cincinnati, Cleveland, Washington, D.C., and 125 other cities throughout the country. One good thing that did come out of those days was the Law Enforcement Assistance Administration (LEAA), which contributed greatly to the professionalism of the police in future years.

It sponsored laws that funded police education and upgrading of equipment and even manpower in many jurisdictions. My old partner, Richie Mason, ultimately earned his master's degree in criminal justice, thanks to LEAA funds.

One additional note of the riot in Plainfield: both George Campbell and Dan Hennessey were among those who testified before the Eastland Senate Judiciary hearings in Washington, D.C., on civil unrest and police response.

CHAPTER EIGHT

Branching Out

Following the riots and during the Officer John Gleason murder investigation, I was assigned by Chief of Detectives Stephen McGlynn to set up an intelligence-gathering project. While I had helped out in a number of murder investigations, my specialty lay more in the gathering of intelligence, as I did during my days with the Plainfield Special Plainclothes Unit. Richie Mason, on the other hand, was the homicide-experienced guy, so he and State Police Detective Tommy Walker delved deeply into the Gleason murder, while I began putting together an intelligence system. I was a packrat; I collected everything I could about black militants from the news media and developed liaisons with other agencies.

Sterling West, a black detective in Linden, worked with me the rest of that 1967 summer. We ushered an informant all throughout the Union County Area trying to buy guns and anticipate the next uprising. We did take a few guns off the streets, but none of the stolen .30 caliber carbines. Ultimately, only a few of those weapons were ever recovered. We identified potential troublemakers and started files on radicals in the New York/New Jersey area.

One night while waiting for our informant, Detective West told me, "I'm really worried about my younger brother. The Marine Corps called my mom last night and said he was among the missing." West's brother was a combat marine in Vietnam, and Sterling talked about him a lot. About two weeks later confirmation came that, indeed, his brother had been killed in action.

Linda and I were the only two white people at the viewing of West's brother in a black funeral home in Linden. It was a very emotional affair with the brother laid out in his dress blues and two black ramrod-straight U.S. Marines bookending the flag-draped coffin. I think those in attendance were surprised we were there, given the times—this was the mid-sixties, following some nasty riots all over the country. Race relations were still edgy and strained. When Sterling introduced us all around, however, the suspicions melted away. We were accepted as mourners like the rest.

A Rock and a Hard Place

Another of our street informants heard of a campground in Colchester, Connecticut, owned by an avowed communist. He overheard a supposed private conversation that black militants from several states around were going up there for meetings. This was a reliable informant, so I called the FBI in Newark and passed that information to them.

A couple of weeks later, two FBI agents walked into our office on the eighth floor in the courthouse and informed Chief McGlynn that they were taking Investigator David Watts for a ride. McGlynn balked. "Whoa! What's this all about?"

The agents said it was confidential, but I would be returned in an hour. So, with no clue as to why the feds wanted me, out the door I went, officiously sandwiched between them. Once we got into their car, they introduced themselves. Ken Venable, the younger one, and an older Italian fellow whose name was lost long ago in the gray matter in the back of my head, got down to business, but now in a much more matter-of-fact manner.

We drove around Elizabeth in the government car. "There will be no reporting of this meeting, David," they explained. "Your information on the Colchester matter was dynamite. Based on your lead, we have been watching that camp. There are dozens of black militant types up there doing the low crawl, shooting rifles in the woods, and having outdoor classes. It looks like a basic training class for revolutionaries. We need more from you."

Agent Venable continued, "Where did you get this information? We gotta follow up on this and we wanna talk to your source. He was right on the money."

Here I was, a young county investigator between a rock and a hard place. I could not and would not reveal my source to anyone. That's standard operating procedure in law enforcement, and they knew it. But the feds are the feds, and they hold a lot of sway. I knew if they went over our heads, right to the county prosecutor, I would be forced to identify our informant. I did my best to reason with them: "If I give him over to you, he will clam up and run for cover. You will get nothing more out of him. Why don't you let Sterling and me give him another try and see if we might be able to milk him a bit longer."

They didn't like it but saw the wisdom in not killing the goose that laid the golden egg. Sterling and I kept after the kid, but he really didn't have anything more and was too afraid to infiltrate the militants. Who could blame him? After all, he only overheard a conversation he was not meant to. Should he now expose that fact to those bad guys? I don't think so.

A funny offshoot of this was young Agent Venable's attempts to sidle up to me for more information. One Sunday he called and invited Linda and me to join him and his wife for a ride in the country. He had a new racy Plymouth Barracuda and wasted no time cranking all the RPMs he could out of it, flying up newly opened Interstate 287. At about 120 mph, Linda leaned over his right shoulder and said, "Hey, FBI big shot, if you don't slow down, I am going to throw up all over your FBI haircut!"

Ultimately, Venable gave up trying to get information out of me by feigning friendship. It was a shallow attempt by the bureau, and we didn't like it.

Lessons from Philly

Chief McGlynn heard that the Philadelphia Police Department had been monitoring black militant activity for many years and had developed protocols to address a variety of challenges presented to law enforcement. They included close personal contact with black leaders, both the legitimate kind and otherwise, outfitting their officers with special riot gear, and the use of buses to rush officers to areas of unrest.

With the prosecutor's blessing, I was assigned by Chief McGlynn to visit Philly's Civil Disobedience Unit, led by Lieutenant George Fencl, an ex-marine. McGlynn's mandate was: "Find out all you can from them, David. Follow Lieutenant Fencl around for a week, and maybe we can help our local towns get a handle on civil unrest."

Fencl ran a tight ship with about a dozen officers, all intensely loyal to him. As luck would have it, while I was there a disorderly mob took over the streets surrounding the Philadelphia Board of Education, which covers a full block of the City of Brotherly Love. Cars were overturned and burned, and upwards of one thousand young black people were doing everything from throwing bricks to burning cars to beating up any white person they came across.

Lieutenant Fencl swung into action. He spoke into his portable radio, "Bus one, deploy on the north side. Bus two, go east and stand by."

Bus one arrived in less than thirty-seconds from its

position just around the corner. Fifty riot police scurried off the bus and quickly formed up in military fashion. They were dressed in black jumpsuits, wore helmets with hard plastic face shields, and carried black batons. Formidable doesn't adequately describe them. They started shuffling down the middle of the street, their boots purposefully scuffing along the blacktop with a rhythmic tempo. The crowd began to fall back. Then Fencl deployed bus two and stood them across an intersection, thus funneling the crowd toward a small park where they ultimately dispersed. I had never seen anything like it.

I saw nationally known civil rights activists there, as well. Father James Groppi, who had the distinction of having been arrested just about everywhere else in the U.S., literally flew past me and into the rear of a police paddy wagon. It may have been unceremonious, but it was an effective way of removing one of the main agitators from the street during the disturbance.

One of Lieutenant Fencl's methods during a demonstration was to personally confront the leader of a group on the street. He would extend his hand, introduce himself, and query the activist as to just what he expected would happen that day. Fencl had a viselike handshake, and you really did not want to be on the receiving end of that greeting. I was next to him when he took the hand of a guy who had been encouraging students to "break some windows and show the pigs we mean it!" The wide-eyed agitator could not pull his hand away as Fencl smiled and pulled him closer, saying, "Listen, you little shit, if this thing of yours breaks bad, I am going to personally put you away for two years—that is, after they release you from Philadelphia General Hospital." The whole hand-crunching time Fencl was smiling, giving the appearance of two buddies sharing a secret. It worked. The guy was thoroughly intimidated and backed off.

I studied the interaction between Fencl's unit and those mob scenes. The unit maintained a balancing act in that no one ever lost their cool in the worst of circumstances. Fencl explained, "This is the result of training, planning, tactics, and follow-through." When Fencl made an announcement to the crowd, no one doubted his resolve. It helped that Mayor Frank Rizzo had his back at every turn. To illustrate: on one occasion I saw Rizzo arrive in his black stretch limo and actually get out with an oversized night stick under his arm. Rizzo might have been mayor of Philadelphia at the time, but he was one of the cops before that. When I got back to the office, my report covered everything I had seen and heard.

Not long after, I had occasion to put some of it to work. An unruly mob in Rahway's downtown section provides an example of the frustrations suffered by police during those years. Rahway Police Chief Herbert Kinch (incidentally, a black man) was on vacation, leaving a white patrol captain in charge of the department. Some store windows were broken, and some minor looting had taken place, but police had the activity confined to a two-block downtown area. The captain had his hands full with both the mob of more than one hundred angry black people and his own frustrated officers. As protocol dictated, the Union County Prosecutor's Office was notified, and Lieutenant Robert Ward told me to stand by in Rahway and give periodic reports to keep the prosecutor up to speed on what was happening.

"David, it's time you put that intelligence stuff to work!" he said.

I arrived at the same time as Detective Pete Diumstra from the intelligence unit of the New Jersey State Police, who was keeping any eye on things for that agency. Imagine me, at twenty-eight years of age, giving advice to senior municipal police officers. Nevertheless, I was representing the prosecutor, and the police respected that.

There was a standoff of sorts, with the cops on one side of the street and a large group of taunting young black people on the other. The captain, Diumstra, and I were talking it over when I noticed one of the older cops jack a shotgun round into the chamber of his .12 gauge. He was a gray-haired, heavy-set guy, probably about ready for retirement, and looked like he had taken all the verbal abuse he was going to from the group across the street. I warned the captain, pointing out the older cop. The captain discreetly dressed down the older fellow and sent him to the rear without his shotgun. There were some tense moments as the captain wrestled with the idea of arresting one of the leaders, but he knew if he went in strong, there would be a scuffle that could lead to bloodshed.

The beleaguered captain lamented, "Here I am, a

captain with a black police chief who decides to take a vacation just when this crap breaks out."

Diumstra and I agreed that the leader had to be removed to restore order, but it would be touchy. The captain said they had just been issued mace as part of their equipment, but no one had ever used it. I suggested that he engage the leader in conversation, and at the right time, take him down with mace and get him out of the area, Philly/Fencl-style. Trooper Diumstra agreed. The captain knew we had his back politically, should things turn bad. Most of the mob didn't even know it when the leader went bye-bye because there was no commotion. It was quiet and quick. The police held fast, and the crowd, sans its agitator mouthing off, gradually dispersed without any further problems.

KEEPING AN EYE ON THINGS

One day I decided to stop in at Plainfield HQ and see how things were going following the riot. Detective Sergeant Patrick McColgan and I had a sit-down upstairs in the bureau. He said things were gradually returning to normal, but that Linward Cathcart was enjoying his newfound public attention and had set up a storefront on West Fourth Street. Cathcart, that self-appointed spokesperson for the blacks, continuously spouted the usual black militant anti-police line. He had gathered a sizable following of impressionable teens from Plainfield's West End, and McColgan considered Cathcart a potential problem.

Cathcart wrote articles for the local paper, and they printed all of them. I thought I should pay him a visit.

The storefront was nondescript with a handmade sign saying something like, "West End Community Council." The front door was unlocked, so I walked in. Dressed in a suit, to any observer in that area, I was obviously law enforcement. The shocked looks on the faces of those inside told me my visit was unexpected and out of the norm. About a dozen black youths were visible throughout the shop, and they glared at me. Against the back wall sat Linwood Cathcart on, believe it or not, a throne. His Sydney Greenstreet chair was raised up in the middle of several African symbols: spears, oblong animal skin shields, and long, feathery plumes. Cathcart, wrapped in a leopard-skin robe, registered surprise at my visit.

"What the hell are you doing in here?" he asked.

"Just thought I would stop in and give you my card. I'm with the Union County Prosecutor's Office, and I can be a friend—that is, if you want one. Yeah, I know, Linward, I'm a cop; but my special assignment is to keep track of things and try to stay ahead of the next insurrection, if you know what I mean. Here's my card. Let's talk sometime."

With that, I turned and walked out, leaving a speechless Cathcart and his juvenile retinue in my wake. He called me a few times, but nothing much developed from it. My visit was just to let him know that his antics weren't intimidating anybody. I'm sure he got the idea he was being watched, and that was a good thing.

THE EQUATION OF POLITICS

Poli (many) + *tics* (blood sucking insects) = politics

Nowhere is government more political than at the county level. Just about everyone is either elected or appointed, so patronage and favoritism prevail. The public is not well served when the primary consideration of an issue is political, rather than simply the right thing to do. I had such an experience during my two-year stint at the Union County Prosecutor's Office.

It was in October 1967, during a lull in the Gleason homicide investigation. Lieutenant Robert Ward called me into his office. "David, I want you to go down to the sheriff's office and look into this. I just got a call that a note passed from one prisoner to another might be evidence in a subornation of perjury case. The one guy asked the other to lie for him in court. Check it out, and start with Sheriff Oriscello, as a courtesy. It's his jail."

I made an appointment with the sheriff on the sixth floor of the tower in the Union County Complex, just three floors below our office. Ralph Oriscello, an ex-Elizabeth police captain, was a tall, swarthy bull of a man. He had a square jaw, hairy arms, and big hands. When we greeted each other, I thought his fingers could go around my hand a second time. He explained, "One of my correction officers intercepted this note and we are supposed to pass this type of thing on to the prosecutor, so here it is."

He handed me the scribbled note, which read, "Tell them you were wrong. I will take care of you."

Sheriff Oriscello explained that inmate George Richard Jacques was scheduled for trial, and the note went to a prisoner who was to testify against him. Actually, the note was passed through a third prisoner, which was how it was intercepted by the corrections officer. I was given clearance to interview the corrections officer, his supervisor, and, of course, the prisoner go-between who tried to pass the note from Jacques to the other inmate.

Before I left the sheriff's office, however, I was treated to a short lecture by Oriscello. "David, this Jacques fellow is a bad one. He disrupts my jail every time he is brought in. He's a real problem for me, if you know what I mean." As he ended that sentence, he leaned forward, his eyes focused on mine, with his head slightly nodding up and down, as if I should be getting what he was trying to convey, but not in so many words. I was slightly taken aback by this display and, at that time, had no idea of his meaning.

I took statements from the corrections officer, the jail warden, and Thomas Edward Tuohy, the inmate Jacques initially gave the note to with a nod to pass it on to Robert McC., the witness for the prosecution against Jacques. Tuohy was a slightly built nervous character who was serving twenty days in the county jail on a gambling conviction. His statement went well. I confirmed the chain of custody of the note through the statements and was about to put a report together recommending a complaint of subordination of perjury against Jacques. Lieutenant Ward stopped me as I passed his door to say

Sheriff Oriscello wanted to see me, so I headed to his office.

"Good morning, Sheriff. You wanted to see me?"

"Yes . . . please sit."

"David, my officers advise me that you have taken statements and might be finishing up your investigation of the Jacques matter. Is that right?"

"Yes," I answered confidently. "Looks like we have a good case against Jacques. All the evidence points to subordination of perjury. I checked the statute, and it seems to be a perfect fit."

The sheriff slowly pushed his chair back from his desk. Frowning, he looked down at his intertwined fingers and said, "David, we have to talk. As I said before, this Jacques guy is a problem for me and my staff. He is about to be released in a week or two. He causes big trouble every time he's in my jail. He led a hunger strike last time. He has no regard for our rules, and his behavior encourages other inmates to act up, as well. Do you get my drift?"

I heard what he had said, and the "drift" seemed to be he wanted me to drop the case against Jacques. I said, "Uh-huh, he's a problem."

"Right. I guess you know what to do."

I sat there frowning, trying to come up with a response. All I could say was, "Ah, well . . ."

Oriscello, his head tilting slightly and eyes narrowing, said, "We do understand each other, don't we? So, what do you want to do here, David?"

All I could muster in my frustration was, "I just

want to do my job, Sheriff."

With that, Oriscello exploded. He shot up from his seat, arms waving, and yelled, "Get out of my office. Go . . . get the hell out!"

I retreated out of the office past his secretary, who would not look up at me. She always greeted me with a smile, but not this time. On my way back to the ninth floor, it began to sink in. Oriscello really wanted me to dump the case against Jacques, just because he didn't want him in his jail. I couldn't believe it—the sheriff, a public official and past police captain to boot, was intimidated by an inmate.

I went directly to Lieutenant Ward's office. Ward looked up, then quipped, "What's up, kid? You look like you just got hit by a truck."

I collapsed into his side chair. "Oriscello just screamed bloody murder at me and kicked me out of his office. I don't know what the hell is going on here, Bob, but I swear, I didn't do anything wrong. I think he was telling me to nix my case against Jacques."

Ward had me go over the entire meeting, word for word. He explained, knowingly, "This is one of those times when discretion is the better part of valor. As you thought, Oriscello wants you to torpedo your investigation because he can't stand the prospect of having Jacques in his jail one moment more than he has to. Oriscello has a rep for being a little touchy—unbalanced, if you ask me—so don't worry about it. You're not the first. Let's go see Leo."

Knowing this was above his pay grade and required

some political finesse, Lieutenant Ward took me to Union County Prosecutor Leo Kaplowitz, a studious-looking man in his early forties with dark-rimmed glasses. Thin, polished, and confident, Kaplowitz was also the master politician. He heard me out and said, "Okay, guys. I'll take care of it. David, you did the right thing by taking this to your lieutenant." That was the extent of the prosecutor's response.

Lieutenant Ward and I returned to our duties, and I was off the hook as far as antagonizing Sheriff Oriscello. But the part of this that annoys me to this day is that George Richard Jacques successfully intimidated the whole justice system in Union County with his antics. Jacques was never charged with subornation of perjury, and the whole ruckus died out. I swallowed hard and moved on.

All this political posturing was new to me. I always thought people said what they meant and meant what they said. This was part of my indoctrination into the real world of give and take, of win a little, lose a little. My naïveté was wearing away.

As an afterthought, you might be interested in knowing that George Richard Jacques, this career criminal, was convicted of first-degree murder in nearby Middlesex County a couple of years later. The victim was shot, execution-style, once in the head and three times in the torso.

ACCIDENTAL P.I.

Part Two:
From Public Service to Private Investigator

CHAPTER NINE

Reevaluation Time

At just about the time of the George Richard Jacques incident, I took a good look around me. I was twenty-nine years old and married for the past seven years to my high-school sweetheart. We still weren't living where we wanted to (who had 20 percent down payment on a house?), and time was passing.

I also took a hard look at the guys I was working with. With the notable exception of Richie Mason, most were heavy drinkers and suffered from depression to one degree or another. I called it the "cop affliction," the five Ds: drunk, divorced, depressed, deluded, and heading for dead. Too many were divorced, and some were so invested time-wise that they were hopelessly locked into hanging in there until retirement. I didn't want that to be me. I also was pissed off at the political environment in the county.

Here's another example of the politics: One day Richie and I got onto the elevator in the courthouse. It was a self-service elevator, but there was an attendant sitting on a high stool to push the buttons for us. Richie turned to me and said, "What if I told you that political appointee sitting there makes $9,000 a year pushing those buttons, while you are making $8,500 a year risking your neck kicking in doors?" My decision to leave the Union County Prosecutor's Office had been germinating, so Richie's observation wasn't lost on me. But where to go and how to do it?

It was a time of indecision for me. I took the exam for the New Jersey State Police and passed the written, the physical, the boxing, and the medical. All that remained was the final interview and completion of the background check. I had long admired the NJSP and thought it might work out for me. Making it even more alluring was a conversation I had with Lieutenant Mike Gooch, head of the NJSP Intelligence Unit, who hinted that after a year or so as a road trooper I might transfer to his unit based on my experiences in Plainfield and at the prosecutor's office. While it was tempting, I realized that another law-enforcement job would put Linda and me in the same box as before, no matter where it was. Instead, I decided to go completely off the reservation and look into insurance investigation. I didn't know much about it, but it had "investigation" in the title, and that was good enough to pique my curiosity.

I drove to Allstate Insurance Company in Murray Hill on a day off from my county job. With no appointment, I confidently walked into the main reception lobby and was greeted by a pleasant fiftyish receptionist. I told her who I was and that I was looking for a career change. I wondered what might be available. She came back with the encouraging information that Allstate was in the market for claims adjusters and they were about to open a big new office to cover Middlesex County. Then she asked me what college I graduated from. My one year at Rutgers studying economics and the Malthusian theory of supply and demand was not going to cut it. She was very kind but said I must have a college degree to apply. Discouraged, I thanked her and began to leave.

Halfway to the door and with nothing to lose, I turned around and said, "You know, that is the dumbest thing I ever heard." Taking a few steps back toward her, I continued, "You mean to tell me that if a recent college grad with no work experience came in, you would take him over someone with eight years of law enforcement and most of it doing detective work? You gotta be kidding!" I was respectful but confident.

The receptionist stared at me for a long moment, blinked a couple times, tapped her pen, and pointed me to a chair. "You sit right there. There's someone you should meet." I sat.

A few minutes later a chubby middle-aged man in a blue suit came out and introduced himself. Earl Buckley, the claims manager, took me into a side interview room and we talked for a while. Then he threw a battery of tests at me, and we spent most of the afternoon, on and off, together. Around four p.m. he came in and said that I was a serious contender and allowed that my investigative experience could bring a valuable perspective to the claims staff in that new office they were about to open in Middlesex County.

Here's the best part: Buckley confided that he was not a college graduate either and that he had done just fine at Allstate without a degree. He promised to sell me to the higher-ups and did just that. Sometimes a little chutzpah at just the right moment goes a long way.

When I offered my resignation to Chief Stephen McGlynn at the prosecutor's office, he did not make a serious effort to dissuade me, but he said he thought someday I would regret my decision. He was wrong. My experience up to that point had prepared me better than any college education could have for what would come later in my life, and I am forever grateful for that, but it was time to move on before my alternatives ran out.

"WELL, IT'S ONLY A CIVIL SUIT"

Having spent eight years investigating everything from fatal accidents to fraud to murder and other forms of mayhem, you would think that moving over to the civil side would be a letdown. It's all too common to overhear a desk sergeant say, "Hey, it's only a civil suit," just after scooting a complaining citizen out the front door of headquarters. Universally, law enforcement looks down on civil matters as being less important than police work.

Certainly there is a demonstrable difference between criminal and civil investigations, but try diminishing the importance of civil cases to someone

- Accidental P.I. -

who has been seriously injured with the opposing side denying liability. Explain how unimportant it is to the victim of identity theft when she can't get credit anymore. Convince a man not to take it to heart that he won't see much of his children because of a negative judgment in a custody case. How about the businessman whose former employees have opened a competing business in violation of a noncompete agreement. You could say of each these examples, "Hey, it's only a civil suit," but do you think any of these victims believe their problems are insignificant compared with a criminal case?

No doubt, the skills I learned in my eight years in law enforcement served me well when I entered the civil side of investigations, but only as a launching platform because there was much more to learn on the civil side. Whereas the police have to present a case with evidence demonstrating their theory of guilt *beyond a reasonable doubt*, in a civil case, it is the *preponderance of evidence* that counts, not beyond a reasonable doubt. That means every civil suit is a matter of one side being more convincing than the other with the evidence at hand. It also means working within a legal structure that allows much more latitude than in criminal cases. Civil may not be as glamorous as a shootout at the OK Corral, but it sure can be the Wild West when it comes to building a case.

In a criminal case the defendant's past criminal history is usually inadmissible, unless, of course, the defendant testifies, a rare occurrence. In a civil case the past history of all parties is not only admissible, but it can also be a crucial aspect of the case. If a plaintiff has filed numerous lawsuits and it can be demonstrated he or she does so habitually, the defense will use that past history against the plaintiff. If the plaintiff in a civil case has a past criminal history, his credibility on the witness stand may be attacked using that information against him. Even one's IRS tax records are fair game. Finally, the goal of a civil suit is the redress of an injury of some type. Its purpose is not to punish, rather, to compel restitution or to "make whole," as far as that is possible. In other words, "You hurt me . . . pay me!"

Surveillance of overstated or fraudulent claimants is a common and effective practice in the defense of certain civil suits, but the plaintiff's lawyer will argue that the evidence obtained doesn't provide a complete depiction of the plaintiff's real circumstance. Again, it is it the preponderance of evidence that carries the day in civil matters.

As we know from watching television and movies, criminal cases are brought forward by the prosecution to punish wrongdoers and set standards intended to dissuade others from committing the same crimes. This divergence of purpose between civil and criminal matters requires a mindset that accommodates each arena of litigation. This is why so many former law-enforcement types have a tough time acclimating to the civil side. I was lucky to have experienced the transition from criminal to civil by working for an insurance company for six years after I left law enforcement and before opening a private-investigation company.

CHAPTER TEN

The "Good Hands" Folks

I started with Allstate as a claims adjuster trainee in October 1968. A whole new world of civil litigation opened up, and it took some adjustment (pun intended). At that time, claims adjusters relied heavily on *contributory negligence* to avoid payment of a claim. The operating theory was if a claimant was just 1 percent at fault, he or she had no way to recover through the courts.

That all changed in the next several years. Hairs were split and *comparative negligence* became prevailing law as part of the new innovative New Jersey auto no-fault system. It was designed to cut down on lawsuits, and to some degree it did.

The "verbal threshold" section of the law pretty much threw out those petty cases that some lawyers tried to make into big deals. Policyholders could choose whether or not to accept the verbal threshold. Of course, their premiums were adjusted accordingly. Paying lower premiums meant a policyholder could not sue another party unless the injuries involved were serious, such as fractures, permanent scarring, or the like. Paying higher premiums allowed the policyholder more flexibility in filing a lawsuit.

I caught on quickly, and after getting my new company-issued Ford, I took over another adjuster's pending files when he was promoted to supervisor. I investigated claims, took witness statements, settled with claimants and their lawyers, and kept up with the rest of the adjusters in terms of productivity. It was well established in the claims department that adjusters worked only a couple of days a week. You could actually get a week's work done in that time on the telephone. Except for calling in to the office twice a day, we were pretty much on our own.

In the beginning I followed everything in the handbook, but it wasn't long before the other adjusters reined me in and I did what was required in two or three days a week, just like them. Allstate was happy with that arrangement, and so was I.

The knowledge I picked up at Allstate was invaluable later on when Linda and I began our private-investigation business. My education all came from practical experience, not from textbooks.

Until joining Allstate, I had not worked much with college-educated people. There weren't many cops with degrees in those years. At first, I felt a little intimidated by them, because they had the degree and I didn't, but it didn't take me long to realize that they were no better or smarter than I and, indeed, had less experience in the real world.

I stayed at Allstate for six years and became a senior claims representative, having refused several attempts to promote me to a desk job. I liked working in the field and enjoyed the independence it brought.

In 1970 our dream of moving from Plainfield came to pass when we rented a newly renovated one-bedroom cottage in Cokesbury, New Jersey. To this day Cokesbury is nothing more than a rural hamlet, a crossroads village in Hunterdon County amid farms and country folks who, while wary of outsiders, eventually took to us—*eventually* meaning about twenty years later.

I joined the North Hunterdon Jaycees, which brought me into contact with some movers and shakers in Hunterdon County. After a few years, I became president of the group and was asked to serve on the Hunterdon Drug Abuse Council because of my experiences on the narcotics squad in Plainfield.

One fellow Jaycee, Jeffrey Martin, was a local real estate lawyer who put me in contact with his senior partner, Raymond Drake. Drake was looking for someone to do title searches, so before I knew it, the rest of my short Allstate workweek was filled up.

What I've learned over the years is that given the contest between truth and honesty versus expediency and profits, the latter duo always wins in the insurance claims industry. Facts are manipulated and embellished to accommodate the desired outcome.

If it was apparent that a claim value fell into a certain range, the adjuster had to be creative. You would never get authorization to settle a claim based on your honest estimate of what it was worth. First, you had to sell it to your immediate superiors. They, in turn, were obligated to come up with arguments why it should settle for less. The higher up the ladder the claim went, the harder it was to get an honest settlement value. Hence, as a mere adjuster, you had to embellish the claim way out of sight just to get reasonable authorization. The adjusters who got promoted were the best at arguing down a claim value, not placing a fair and honest value on it. Also, you had to lie to the trial lawyers, arguing that you had no more authorization and the claim wasn't worth it. If you really wanted to settle a claim, you were caught between the trial lawyer who was overselling it and the claim bosses who were underselling it. It was a con game, but with real lives at stake. If you played their game, you were favored; if not, well, you were not a team player. In my mind, this went far beyond legitimate negotiation.

By the time I left Allstate in 1974, I learned well how to game the system and have things turn out the way the company wanted. I am not singling out Allstate. In my contacts with other companies, I found the whole insurance claims industry operated that way, and it troubled me.

Of course, all this happened forty years ago. My understanding is that many of the practices that Allstate and others engaged in then have since changed. Nevertheless, and for all its faults, Allstate has always been an icon of the claims industry. So now, in my early thirties, I had worked for two widely accepted professional organizations: Plainfield Police and Allstate Insurance Company. This was a really good start!

After a while, the combination of my Allstate responsibilities and title searching became too much. I felt like I had one foot on a boat and the other on the dock— and the boat was moving. I was feeling the "stretch" and had to make a choice. I also learned something about myself. I wasn't suited for the corporate world. It's not that I am not a team player; rather, I just cannot put up with arrogant incompetents who seem to know everything by virtue of their positions and are not open to suggestions from the trenches where most of the work is done. Wait a minute—I guess I am not a team player, after all.

CHAPTER ELEVEN

Moving into Uncharted Territory

Over time, at Allstate and other insurance companies, road adjusters became dinosaurs, replaced by telephone adjusters, usually recent college graduates. The companies didn't have to pay for the company cars and higher salaries of the more experienced road adjuster, but the quality of claims handling fell off. What the insurance companies should have done was to keep a sensible mix of road and desk adjusters working in harmony with one another.

I have never been one for the status quo. I believe in working hard and being responsible for my own condition. I have a hard time working for people who toe the company line even when it is obviously counterproductive. So it's not surprising that I had a problem with the fact that Allstate accepted the two-day workweek, as long as the claims adjusters produced. Basically, it was a racket. I was getting tired of getting by with a cushy job with time passing and no hope of getting up in the world.

I finally handed in my resignation at Allstate, and

Linda and I were off and running in our own title-search business. This happened on precisely the same day (June 6, 1974) we undertook our first home mortgage. Ray Drake, the attorney for whom I had been doing title searches, had arranged for a private land mortgage on a 2.5-acre piece of property in Cokesbury, where we built a 1,400-square-foot ranch. Drake was one of many mentors along the way who believed in us and held open a door of opportunity. Opportunity does knock, but you have to have the good sense to recognize it and the guts to act when it comes along.

Title searching gave us our first taste of entrepreneurial experience. Linda and I worked well together. We learned how to title search the old-fashioned way by slinging those large tomes at the courthouse and plotting the various courses, finishing up with a sketch that represented the metes and bounds description of real property. We soon merged our startup business with Jim Pence, a friendly competitor, and began writing title insurance policies for Commonwealth Land Title Insurance Company, which is based in Philadelphia and actually invented title insurance. Times were good. Being our own boss was the ticket—a chance to make a life for ourselves.

Another mentor, Bob Hartlaub, entered the picture. He had started out as a milkman and finished as vice president of Commonwealth Land Title Insurance Company. No one in the title industry had more clout than Hartlaub, and he took a liking to Team Watts.

"Can you plot a metes and bounds description?" he asked soon after we met.

"Of course," I replied. "How do you do a sixty-year search without knowing where it is in relation to adjoining property, and how would you identify exceptions?"

Our first face-to-face meeting with Hartlaub was at his office in Summit. At that time, he was president of his own company, Crestview Lawyers Service, and owned the building as well. He was impressed with Linda's blunt approach, since his was the same.

"Do you own this building?" she asked.

"Yes, I do, Linda." Hartlaub was seated behind his desk in his fancy corner office with a large photo of an antique Indian motorcycle on the wall. He might have been a successful businessman, but he never forgot his roots. He rode his Harley whenever he could.

"Well," Linda remarked, "you should know that the second toilet in the ladies room is leaking."

Hartlaub looked from Linda to me and back, then laughed. "I will have to look into that," he said. He liked plain-talking people. He sent us all his Warren County business and supported us any way he could. At our open house for our Washington, New Jersey, office, he arrived with a retinue of his own employees so that our party would have enough people present to avoid embarrassment. To his surprise and delight, however, we did pretty well on our own and had all the local lawyers and their paralegals drinking punch and munching on chips when he got there.

Hartlaub loved our spunk. When the fees for municipal tax and assessment searches were raised from $6 to $20 each, we had to front the cost of each search until the real-estate deal closed and money was dispersed. At times we were putting out several hundred dollars on tax and assessment searches while waiting for a closing. So, Linda and I sent a letter to all our lawyer clients indicating when they ordered a search, they should submit appropriate checks made out to the tax collector and assessor, which we would then forward. Why should we be depleting cash flow while carrying law firms for these fees? Our competitors thought we were nuts. "Self-destructive," they called it. "Lawyers will never go for that." But to everyone's surprise, they did. Consequently, we preserved cash flow and, at the same time, gained respect from all concerned. Team Watts was catching on to doing business.

Using our partner Jim Pence's back title files, we were able to make inroads in Warren County and soon became the alternative to Chelsea Title & Guarantee, the largest and for years the most successful agency in the area. Hard work and perseverance paid off. For the first time in our lives, we were in charge of our own destiny.

CHAPTER TWELVE

Scratching that Itch

After some time in the title-search business, that old "investigation itch" began gnawing at me. I longed for something more than investigation of land titles. Title searching had been profitable and even interesting in a historical sense, but I missed the dynamic interaction of people and their problems. I decided to add private investigation to our business, just to see how that would work. I had the qualifications: a minimum of five years of law-enforcement experience and a clean record.

I received my first private-detective license in spring 1976. As I drove away from the New Jersey State Police Headquarters in West Trenton, I peeked at my new private investigator's ID card and knew I was going to be happy back in the investigation saddle.

Linda and I ran the title business and the fledgling investigation business out of the same office in Washington, New Jersey. I was able to convince a few local trial lawyers to give my investigative skills a chance.

Attorney Bill Albrecht, a former FBI special agent,

gave us a chance and liked our investigation work. He referred us to his main office in Morristown. That firm, Schenck, Price, Smith & King, was outside counsel for Selected Risks Insurance Company. We began doing surveillance for the insurance company on overstated and fraudulent claims. This fit well with my experience. Surveillance came naturally from my detective days, and now, because of my time at Allstate, I spoke the language of insurance adjusters, as well.

Linda, who is a great one for detail and thoroughly enjoys the historical nature of the old deeds and mortgages, was doing well with the title-searching business and loved it. Gas shortages and the mortgage crunch at the time put a crimp in the real estate market, however, and the slowdown of house sales trickled down to title searching. We approached our junior partner, Jim Pence, to buy us out. He is still in business today successfully operating Probe Lawyer's Service, the name of our first company.

Somewhere along the way, Linda began going on surveillance with me. She turned out to be a very good motion-picture photographer. She held the camera (Super 8mm in those days, video later on) steady and resisted the urge to zoom in and out as so many amateurs do. We bought a used 1976 Dodge Maxivan from my barber in Hackettstown, New Jersey, and used it on many surveillances for insurance companies and their lawyers. We would roll out of bed at four a.m., and while Linda would put together lunch, I would load that aircraft carrier-sized van and off we would go into the sunrise.

By about six a.m., we would be sitting on surveillance together in some town in Morris, Hudson, Union, Passaic, Bergen, or any other northern New Jersey county, arriving early enough to catch claimants on their way to jobs they had denied having in sworn depositions. We caught them lifting, running, hammering, bending, and doing myriad activities that they swore in their answers to interrogatories and depositions that they could no longer do. We were good at it, and the word began to spread. Then came another big break.

Archie Magliochetti, one of my former bosses at Allstate, had just been put in charge of commercial claims. He called with a big case he wanted us to take on. The Freeman & Bass law firm in Newark had dumped 508 workers' compensation petitions in Allstate's lap. The petitions claimed workplace sickness caused by toxicity in the air at Topper Toy, a factory in Elizabeth, New Jersey. The plant had closed eight years before, and our job was to identify intervening employment for those claimants. If Allstate found the claimants were engaged in subsequent work in a similar environment, then the current insurance company would pick up 80 percent of the workers' compensation claim and Allstate would have to pay only 20 percent, so it was worth paying for a thorough investigation of each claim to come up with that information.

We worked on that case for the better part of three years and saved Allstate about $1.5 million in claims payments. Thanks to Archie Magliochetti, this first big case gave us the breathing room to establish ourselves.

The Allstate investigation required fieldwork in some hostile urban areas, so we hired Humberto Granada, a Cuban and former undercover cop. He had been involved in the Bay of Pigs fiasco and came highly recommended by my old partner at the Union County Prosecutor's Office, Richie Mason. We leased a little yellow Plymouth Arrow for Granada and set him loose in Elizabeth and Newark.

He would step onto the claimant's porch carrying a clipboard and go into his act: "I am here to repossess the sewing machine." The claimant would invariably deny that Granada had the right person, and a discussion clarifying the claimant's identity would ensue. It worked beautifully. Granada would identify where the person worked. If the job was in the same type of work environment as Topper Toy, then it would push 80 percent of that claim onto the insurance company of the current employer. Allstate loved it. Reliance Insurance, the carrier that turned up most frequently, hated it.

One day Granada called quite upset. "Davie, what do I do with this sewing machine I just took from a little old Haitian lady? When I did my thing on her porch, she handed over her sewing machine and said, 'Da goddam ting don work right anyhow, mon!'"

GROWING THE ENTERPRISE

Our reputation for consistent good investigation work spread among insurance companies, and we began to hire helpers. One of the first was Bob Becker, a recent college grad and friend of the family. He worked for us for about a year between college and law school. He is now a respected trial lawyer in Albuquerque, New Mexico.

Many young criminal justice majors passed through our company on their way to their dream "alphabet job" (FBI, DEA, ATF, INS). Some were more notable than others, but Becker was the best.

In 1976, just after I got my P.I. license, I bought a book, *The Legal Investigator*, by Anthony Golec. Halfway through it, I stopped, found Golec in Illinois, and gave him a call. I joked, "You son of a gun, you wrote my book!" Everything in that book was what I had learned along the way in police work, at Allstate, and, yes, even title searching.

At Golec's urging, we joined the National Association of Legal Investigators (NALI) and for the next fifteen years attended seminars around the country. We met other private investigators who also preferred to be known as "legal investigator," rather than private detective or private investigator. The idea was to elevate the profession from the film-noir portrayals of the thirties and forties. I held several offices in NALI over the years, but, as usual, Linda did all the grunt work. She got the job and I got the glory.

In 1989 we sponsored the NALI Annual National Conference and Seminar in Philadelphia, which drew more than three hundred attendees.

Dr. Michael Baden, former chief medical examiner for New York City and currently a Fox News contributor, was one of the conference speakers in Philadelphia. He had just finished his book, *Unnatural Death—Confessions of a Medical Examiner*, and wanted to promote it at our seminar. In the hours before he spoke, I bought his book and he signed it for me: "Dear David, I hope you enjoy Unnatural Death!" My hope is that he meant the book and nothing more sinister.

Our helper at the Philadelphia conference was Bruce Snyder, an investigator from Lansdale, Pennsylvania. He tells a story that is worth repeating. Like us, Snyder did not like working on marital cases and turned these requests down regularly. On one occasion a man called and said that he wanted to hire Snyder to follow his wife. Snyder explained that he didn't do that kind of work and gave the man the name of another investigator who would, but the man was insistent. He said that he had heard of Snyder's reputation and wanted him, personally, on the case. Again, Snyder refused. This went on back and forth for more than a week.

One morning Snyder arrived at his office to find the man sitting on the front step waiting for him. Snyder walked inside and down the hall, the man right on his heels. Snyder, frustrated by now, was trying to get the man to leave him alone. All the while the guy kept pleading. Finally, once seated behind his desk Snyder looked up at the man standing in front of him, about to tell him off. The man leaned over, pen in hand, and said, "Here is a check for $10,000, and I want you start this weekend." Snyder replied, "Sir, you have my undivided attention!"

We usually sent our marital and custody cases to Bob Higgins, a retired New Jersey State Police sergeant. He always did a great job and worked with us on many other cases over the years, as well. Of course, there were times when a well-heeled client would have "our undivided attention" and we would keep that case in-house. Higgins understood and remains our close associate to this day.

They Grabbed the Kid . . .

One of our earliest cases was a domestic kidnapping. The mother and her boyfriend came to our office in a hysterical state. They explained that the child's father had joint custody of the six-year-old boy but did not return him as required. The couple reported this to the county authorities and the local police but were not satisfied everything was being done to get the boy back.

When someone plans to run away, the key is to learn as much as possible about the person to come up with reasonable search alternatives. I interviewed the boy's mother for a couple of hours. We identified all of the relatives and friends we possibly could, filling up page after page of a legal pad. The father had a stepsister in Florida, but the child's mother said, "There's no way he would go there. They never got along. No way!"

We continued the discussion. The volume of information was building up and becoming unwieldy. There were several parties I thought could be involved, so I mentioned them to the mother. She was wishy-washy most of the time, but whenever I mentioned the stepsister in Florida, she was adamant: "I told you . . . no way he would go there. They argue all the time, and he doesn't like her at all."

The father's brother owned a gas station in Rahway and the mother thought they would be in close contact, but there was no way he would give his brother up. I sent Eddie Micali, one of my part-timers, to the station with a clipboard and a hand counter. He was to sit in the station and monitor traffic on the nearby road. The phony story we gave the brother was that the highway department was considering changing the lane pattern in the area, which would result in two lanes eastbound on the gas station's side and one on the other. This supposed change would benefit the station owner. The brother went for it, and Micali sat in the station not far from the phone.

This went on for four days, and then came our break. One of the mechanics answered the phone and yelled into the bay, "Hey, boss, it's your brother."

The brother answered, "Tell him I'll call him back."

On the callback, Micali was able to pick up parts of the conversation that indicated the missing boy was at the stepsister's house in the Miami area. This is the same stepsister that didn't get along with the child's father. Sure.

I called a NALI member in Miami and asked him to cruise by the stepsister's trailer early the following Sunday. Sure enough, the father's New Jersey car was parked in the drive.

Armed with this information, the mother and her

boyfriend flew to Miami and did some surveillance on their own. When the stepsister and her husband walked across a mall parking lot with the boy in tow, the mother and her boyfriend intervened. They recovered the child, but not before planting a black eye on the stepsister's husband.

They were smart. Instead of rushing directly to Miami International, they drove north to Fort Lauderdale and boarded a flight to Atlanta, then changed to another airline for the flight back to New Jersey.

There was a lesson in this case for us. Our clients were sure that the child's father would not go to his stepsister's house in Florida, yet that's what happened. I learned that when a scenario is "so impossible" (as in the mother's responses), it is one of the first things to check. No doubt, when the father kidnapped the boy, he knew the boy's mother would never suspect his plan to go to his stepsister in Florida.

ENTERING THE CORPORATE WORLD

John Mallon, one of my radio car partners back in Plainfield, stayed with the department long enough to be promoted to lieutenant. But then like some of the rest of us, Mallon decided to make a change. He landed a job as security manager at Johnson & Johnson headquarters in New Brunswick, New Jersey, where he worked directly for Jim Atkinson, director of corporate security for J&J and its 150 or so companies. In 1985 Mallon, hearing we were doing well with our private investigation business, called on us. Our subsequent work for J&J gave us added credibility in the corporate world, and other major corporations followed.

We joined the American Society for Industrial Security at Mallon's suggestion. Soon we were working for Procter & Gamble in Cincinnati, Lockheed Government Electronics Systems in South Jersey, and, of course, the local J&J companies in and around Central Jersey. They were always great cases and there was never a question of cost. Ask any investigator, and there's no arguing: the best clients are the Fortune 500.

Patrick J. Keefe was the security manager at Ortho Pharmaceuticals (one of J&J's companies) in Raritan, New Jersey, and Mallon referred us to Keefe for investigations. Our first meeting was less than auspicious. We had just finished up an assignment for Al Payne, Keefe's assistant, when I met with them both in their Raritan office to go over our findings. I began with a short introduction to the case when Keefe tersely interrupted, "Is this going to be long? I have an important meeting scheduled."

I knew that the corporate folks operate in a "pecking order" atmosphere and that Keefe was just asserting his dominance. But I also knew that unless I responded appropriately, I would be bowled over by his forceful personality and forever be at that disadvantage. With a hint of a sarcastic smile, I came back, "It won't take long at all. Hey, it's your money. If you aren't interested in the results you are paying me for, maybe I should just send in the report and not bother coming in to explain the nuances."

It worked. Keefe smiled, softened his tone, and we got down to business. I must say, he turned out to be one of our best corporate clients, as well as a business cheerleader on our behalf. Over the years we became fast friends, as well.

While it would be out of bounds to discuss most of those cases, there is one I can relate without breaking any confidences. Keefe called me at our office one day around three p.m. "Come to my office and pick up two airline tickets. You and Linda are going to San Juan, Puerto Rico, on the midnight flight tonight." Ortho has a plant in Puerto Rico, and plant manger Juan Arruza had called Keefe requesting assistance. While the problem might seem a bit trivial, it was taken quite seriously by Arruza. The San Juan plant consists of several acres under roof, and loudspeakers located throughout the building's steel rafters were disappearing. Keefe said that he had other commitments but wanted to demonstrate that corporate cared enough to respond promptly and professionally. We were elected.

When we arrived at four thirty a.m., we were exhausted. Arruza called our hotel room at seven thirty a.m. I decided to pull a Pat Keefe on him and said, "We just got in. I'll meet you in the lobby at ten," then hung up. Hey, if I am standing in for Mr. Keefe, I might as well go all-out Keefe.

Arruza took me to the plant, and, along with our

interpreter, Police Lieutenant Jaime Gonzalez, we began interviewing employees. I acted the nasty white gringo from the home office while Gonzalez interpreted. We got nothing from any of the employees. I thought there must be another way. As in most investigations, when you come up against a stone wall, you start over, but from a different perspective. I asked to take a tour of the plant's rafters to see the remaining speakers. After inspecting the speakers, I had an idea.

"Mr. Arruza, when I look on the back of these speakers I see that they can operate both on plant current and twelve volts. Would that mean they can be used as speakers in cars?" Both Arruza and his maintenance man stared at each other for a moment, a dim light beginning to appear. "Yes, they can," replied the maintenance man.

"Let's take a walk in the employee parking lot," I suggested.

It didn't take long to spot these large speakers lined up in the rear windows of a number of employee cars. Problem solved. After that, Arruza and his wife took us out to celebrate. Arruza was happy. Keefe was happy. Linda and I were happy to have had the experience, but most of all to be back home.

Keefe left Ortho to become director of corporate security for Colgate Palmolive Company in New York and took us with him as outside investigators. Later he was promoted to vice president of security worldwide for Colgate and its subsidiaries. The investigation jobs kept coming our way.

We participated in security for the Colgate Women's

Games in the old Madison Square Garden. Our part was executive protection of the big shots and their families during that event. Keefe and I were walking around the outer-ring hallway when an NYPD detective ran by with his gun out and yelling into his radio. Just then Colgate's CEO, Rubin Mark, walked up as another NYPD cop stopped and told us there had been shots fired on the floor below. We radioed our troops to close ranks on their assignees, then Keefe and I grabbed Mark by each elbow and literally carried him through the nearest door, marked "Women." When the "all clear" was radioed, the CEO of Colgate hugged Keefe in appreciation right there in the women's room.

An Overreaching Claimant

Keefe assigned us surveillance of an employee who was out of work because of an injury on the job. In his workers' compensation claim, he alleged that he could no longer reach his hands and arms above his head, among several other physical complaints. What made the case all the more sensitive was the claimant was an out-spoken African American councilman in a nearby city.

We followed the subject for a few days and finally hit pay dirt. The employee parked in a municipal parking lot and went into a nearby workout center. I went inside and saw him riding one of the stationary bikes and sweating up a storm. I went back to the van to grab my Minox camera and went back in. Using the mirror, I was able to get still photos of him lifting heavy weights above his head repeatedly.

Keefe now had evidence that controverted the employee's physical disability claim. Obviously, the man had recovered from his injury and was milking the case for all he could.

UNDERCOVER IN THE ANIMAL RIGHTS MOVEMENT

We had a particularly fascinating case involving an investigation of the animal rights movement. We were hired by a consortium of other corporate clients who will remain anonymous for obvious reasons. We managed to insert four undercover operatives into several animal rights groups in three states and reported their intentions back to our clients. We carefully documented these organizations and their members for three years. Our efforts defeated several serious attacks on company laboratories and high-level corporate meetings, as well as a number of incidents that would have caused public embarrassment for our clients and other companies. Some of our work was shared with law-enforcement agencies.

On one occasion our corporate client had scheduled a shareholder's meeting where it was feared that animal activists would try to disrupt the gathering of approximately five hundred attendees. Our undercover operatives learned that the plan was to use local college students to gain access to the meeting by applying for temporary jobs as ushers. Once in, they would begin yelling obscenities, then throw animal blood on the shareholders.

This information was called in by our undercover just an hour before the program got under way, so time was of the essence. The security director acted quickly once we notified him of the activists' plan. He took the manager of the facility aside and asked if he had hired any last-minute ushers. The manager admitted he was short-handed and did indeed hire four young men earlier that day. The four were gathered together and dismissed on the spot. Bottles of blood were located just outside one of the emergency exits. The financial investment that the corporate group made in our undercover project paid off that time.

In another situation, our undercover operative learned that a small group of animal rights activists intended to block traffic at the entrance of a company along a busy road in the New Brunswick, New Jersey, area. They planned to arrive via pickup truck just before the morning rush hour at the plant's entrance, where, with their rubber boots encased in heavy cement blocks, they would stand in the way of traffic until they were arrested. The whole idea was for the media to cover the traffic tie-up, thus allowing them to get their message across: "No animal testing."

We had to decide whether or not to take action. If we thwarted the operation, our operative's cover would likely be blown. There was a great deal of head scratching over this one, but the decision to do nothing was necessary.

Our undercover's position in the group had been nurtured for more than a year, and we did not want to risk losing the intelligence we were receiving almost daily. Of course, safety of our operative was paramount, as well.

As predicted, when the day arrived the morning rush hour was a tangle of snarled traffic backed up for miles in the New Brunswick area. Thankfully, our undercover was safe and delivered much more information as time went on. Sometimes you just have to weigh the consequences and accept the lesser of two evils.

There were many other times when our undercover investigators provided valuable intelligence to our clients, thus preventing serious criminal acts and, no doubt, protected corporate interest. But of more significance, our investigative services protected the physical safety of company employees.

"What the Heck . . . Our Numbers Are Up."

In the corporate world the only thing that counts is the numbers. The score. The means by which success is measured, whatever that is. In sales, it's achieving goals and making the cut. The so-called Fortune 500 all have marketing and sales staffs that live or die by the numbers. They either reach their projected goals or they are failures. This self-induced pressure is tremendous, and internal competition runs rampant.

Enter *product diversion*. This little-known crime is perpetrated against large corporations by unscrupulous business entrepreneurs who understand and take advantage of the weakness of marketing/sales practices. What is worse, this corruptive practice could not exist without the complicity of the company.

Let me explain. Company A has an overrun of widgets and decides to dispose of them by donating them or selling them at a drastically reduced price to a third-world country.

Or Company B decides to enter the Bulgarian widget market and, with advance research, styles the product to the liking of the average Bulgarian.

Or Company C comes up with the idea of donating a welcome package of their widgets to kids just entering college as a means of establishing a future generation of widget buyers.

In all three cases, these widgets are not intended to enter the American marketplace. Obviously, if they did, they would undermine everyday widget business because they are either free or grossly underpriced for their intended market. The widget manufacturer would be competing against itself. How smart would that be?

To facilitate these transactions, the companies engage a third party to act as the distributor. Therein lies the problem. The widget manufacturer doesn't want to be involved with the minutiae of getting widgets to college campuses or Bulgaria, for that matter. Realizing the potential inherent in the price differential, certain profiteering distributors promise to fulfill the contract and expedite shipping, etc. of tractor-trailer loads of widgets to wherever.

The widgets, however, never get to their intended destinations. Instead, the widgets turn up in dollar stores, bodegas, and flea markets around the country, providing tremendous profits to the illegal distributors, called *diverters*. In fact, these product-diversion schemes costs companies millions of dollars.

So, why don't the companies just stop the whole mess by not dealing with the diverters? Why don't they recognize the problem and deal with it? The answer is in the numbers. Often, this is how the sales staff meets its goals and keeps its numbers up.

Those extra trailer loads of widgets leaving the plant save many a sales rep's rep. As counterintuitive as this may seem, it is common practice. There seems to be a disconnect between the upper echelon who should be interested in the company's bottom line and those in sales who are interested only in their own bottom lines. There is, however, a delicate balance between these two entities. Those at the top want good numbers, too, so more often than not the diverters get away with it.

Now, here comes the security department. Once security professionals get wind of it, they try to prove the diversion is taking place and the contract is being violated. An investigation is initiated. We have worked on many of these types of cases requiring undercover work and surveillance. Sometimes, the legal department gets involved, and a federal lawsuit is brought against the diverter. No problem. They just give in, then open up under another name and approach the same sales department with a phony new idea to "project company reach." The sales department goes for it all over again. It's nuts!

In one of our product-diversion cases, the security manager of a well-known corporation called me to explain that his company had just entered into an agreement to supply colleges and universities with its product, and product diversion was suspected. Our job was to follow the load to its destination, no matter where that took us. The security man had convinced his packaging department to use a very shiny shrink-wrap on the pallets, making them easy to spot on a loading dock.

We set up surveillance at a warehouse in Brooklyn, New York. Investigator Bob Higgins and Matt Orr, one of our younger staff members, used two minivans and kept eyes on the warehouse loading platform until they were able to see the shiny pallets being loaded onto a trailer. When they radioed it in, I called the client and said we were set to follow the load and would keep him apprised.

Our investigators followed the truck out of the warehouse and to the ramp leading up to the Verrazano Bridge when a fortuitous thing happened. The truck driver had a minor accident with another vehicle. During the subsequent police investigation, Higgins went up to the driver and said, "Hey, man, I saw that happen. I'm a driver, too. It wasn't your fault. That woman changed lanes right into you."

In the following conversation, Higgins learned that the load was on its way to Detroit. I called the client, who requested that we continue the surveillance right to the load's final destination.

Linda and I summoned two more of our staff to get ready to join the surveillance, as Higgins would drop off once the load passed our location in Clinton, New Jersey. When the team got close, Orr, in the other van, sped up and got off to gas up. Our new crew then fell in behind the truck, as Higgins fell back. We literally took over the gas station at Clinton's west end, and when Matt pulled in it was like an Indy car refueling. I think he was back on the road in under two minutes and the gas station attendant was a sawbuck richer for his cooperation.

Our guys followed the truck all the way to the headquarters of Supreme Distributors in Detroit. Supreme was a widely known product diverter, and our investigation validated the client's suspicion that this load was not going where it was intended.

A side note: Orr described an incident during that trip when he took a wrong turn and ended up on another interstate going away from our other van and the truck they were tailing. He said he put the pedal to the metal after making an illegal turn across the grass median in an attempt to regain the surveillance. The state trooper who pulled Orr over was cooperative once Orr explained the situation and produced his investigator identification. In fact, the trooper offered to pull the truck over and search it for us. Orr said, "No, that's all right, but I just need to get back up with them." The trooper said, "Follow me!" Orr's minivan had all it could do to keep up with the trooper as he pushed other traffic aside, getting Orr back on track. Our young criminal justice majors loved their work, as you can imagine.

A LITTLE WORLD TRAVELING, TOO!

None other than Allstate sent us to Spain on a case. Bob Brown, an Easton, Pennsylvania, lawyer who handled Allstate's claims, called and advised that a local chiropractor had filed a lawsuit when he tripped and fell over a raised sidewalk in front of the Allstate insured's house. The lawyer suspected this was an overstated claim and had learned that the chiropractor was about to take a vacation in Torremolinos on Spain's Costa del Sol on the Mediterranean Sea.

We contacted the Torremolinos Police and got hooked up with an interpreter who took on odd jobs such as ours. We didn't really need his interpreter service; rather, we needed him to set up the job for us. In short order, he located the plaintiff chiropractor's condo in a complex known as La Playa. Further, our Spanish friend found the rental company where the chiropractor rented his little red Ford Fiesta. We were all set with the condo location, car description, and license plate.

We flew Iberia Airlines to Malaga, rented a car, and drove along the Mediterranean coastline to Torremolinos. For the next two weeks we followed the plaintiff all around the area and videotaped his activities. He would walk for miles with no apparent difficulty. He went about his daily routine quite sure that he was safe from anyone on the other side of his lawsuit and the other side of the pond.

One day he entered a real estate office. He spoke Italian, while the realtor spoke Spanish. Somehow, they managed to understand each other. I stood nearby at the counter reviewing the brochures all the while. In spite of my high school Spanish, I couldn't understand either of them, and when I returned to the car Linda asked, "So what did you learn in there?"

"I learned that real estate is an international language and I need to take that course."

The only worry we had during that job was the Guardia Civil. That is the premier police force in Spain, and they are all business. They work in pairs and carry Uzi-like machine pistols hung out in the open from their shoulders. My concern was that one of them might spot us with our video camera up and running and pull us in for questioning. When we are challenged back home, there's no problem because we are licensed and can prove it. I doubted that our P.I. license would impress the Guardia Civil very much, so we were extra careful when on that job.

Upon our return, Linda and I were deposed by Bob Brown's opposing counsel, Gus Melitis, a well-known and highly successful plaintiff's attorney in Easton, Pennsylvania. I guess we did all right, because the case settled for Allstate's figure, but what took place a couple of months later told the real story.

Linda and I were having dinner in the Clinton

House when Melitis tapped me on the shoulder. He said in a voice loud enough to be heard at nearby tables, "If ever again I get these two investigators against me in a case, I will settle quick as I can. I don't ever want to have them as witnesses again." It felt good to be respected by such a high flyer.

I can't let another funny story go by. While in Spain for that couple of weeks, we took a day off and drove up to Mijas, a small mountaintop village an hour's ride from our hotel. The buildings were whitewashed, the streets were lined with old cobblestones, and the local priest walked around in his cassock looking like a sixteenth-century monk. The swallows flew in and out of the bell tower next to the bullring. It was like stepping back in time. Very bucolic.

As we walked downhill toward the center of town, Linda suddenly remarked, "Uh-oh. A bird just pooped on my blouse." We were getting close to an open-air restaurant where a young waiter was standing with a towel over his arm. He watched us walk up and began staring at Linda's blouse, which by now gave evidence supporting the fact that the transgressing bird must have had a bountiful lunch.

I mustered up my best Spanish (for those of you who speak fluent Spanish, forgive me), "Perdoname, señor. Mi esposa tiene una problema. Un ave hace mierda en la camisa de mi esposa. Ayudame, por favor." The whole time I am struggling to get this message out, the waiter is staring at me, his eyes squinting, and I am thinking my

Spanish really stinks.

When I'm done, the waiter responds, "Listen, mister, I just got here two weeks ago from Brooklyn. I don't know what the hell you said, but did you know a bird crapped on your wife's blouse?"

CHAPTER THIRTEEN

Whitney Houston Cases

No, your eyes are not deceiving you. The chapter title is real. We did work for Whitney Houston through her lawyer, Tom Weisenbeck, when matters arose that went beyond contract issues. Weisenbeck called upon us to do the fieldwork in those cases. While we never met with Whitney, I did meet John Houston, her father, during an investigation of a man who was trying to extort money from the family.

Attorney Weisenbeck and John Houston met with the supposed extortionist while I and former trooper Bob Higgins, both armed, stood by in the next hotel room listening at the adjoining door. Weisenbeck had us bug the room for sound, which is legal in New Jersey—the proviso being the one doing the recording has to be part of the conversation. That was Tom Weisenbeck in this instance.

I suggested that we have the Houston limousine pick up the suspect at the airport when he flew in from Detroit. This would lessen the possibility of his access to any weapons. We recorded the whole conversation, but the man was careful not to say anything that would constitute a crime, and the whole thing died away.

When Whitney's brother, Robert, was arrested in East Orange for drugs, resisting arrest, and assault on a police officer, Weisenbeck tasked me with conducting interviews and getting statements in the local bar where this took place. I hired a recently retired black East Orange police officer and we went into the place together. Once it became clear that I was there to help the younger Houston, the bartender and several patrons could not have been more helpful. Ultimately, the police dropped the more serious charges and, in turn, our attorney dropped the police brutality complaint against the two black officers who gave Robert Houston a good going over that night.

Another Houston case involved two young men who boldly sauntered into Tiffany's in New York City representing themselves as Whitney Houston's assistants. They actually conned this world-famous jewelry store out of five expensive pieces of jewelry, which were put on Whitney's store charge account. With the help of hidden cameras and a phone number foolishly left behind by one of these characters, we identified them and tracked them down to a house in Union County, New Jersey. The police took over our surveillance and arrested the pair later that day.

WHAT COLLEGE DOESN'T TEACH

We continued to grow as a company. By the time we

sold the business in 1998, we had ten full-time field
investigators, a secretary, four outfitted surveillance vans,
two more vehicles, and many associate agencies helping
us manage our continuous caseload of more than two
hundred files at any given time. Our field guys moved
their vans in close and got steady video evidence that
brought about many negotiated settlements. They even
had the opportunity to testify in depositions and trials.

The young college grads we hired had a lot to learn.
Linda and I rode them hard because we knew lawyers on
the other side of these cases were not playing softball.
Linda kept after them about using the right wording in
reports. We used to get "You know what I meant" from
them; but they had to learn that opposing counsel would
tear them apart in depositions or at trial. Then one day
they would see the light.

Two of them were scheduled for a deposition
relating to surveillance videotape they took of an insurance
claimant performing activity that ran contrary to her claim
allegations. Their excellent video evidence left little doubt
that the plaintiff in that case was overstating her case, but
our boys were about to learn that it was not enough to
show the videotape, then sit back and gloat. The plaintiff's
attorney took his shot at the investigator witnesses. Every
word, every action they took, every decision they made
came under scrutiny. They were put through the ringer.
There's nothing like a pissed-off plaintiff's attorney ripping
into you and trying to convince the jury that we were the
big bad investigators that spy on innocent claimants. This

is especially true if you have produced evidence that really hurts the plaintiff's case. There is an axiom in the legal profession: if you can't win on the evidence, attack the witness.

Our guys learned a lesson that day. Their four years of college had done nothing for their ability to survive a grilling by a competent trial lawyer. Everyday experiences and our constant cajoling gave them the tools to survive in the hardball world of civil litigation. Today three of our former field guys operate their own successful investigation agency in Pennsylvania.

Ultimately, we sold our New Jersey investigation business and came out of it whole. We would have liked to have sold it to our employees and we tried to work out a deal to do so. Unfortunately, the negotiations broke down and some hard feelings resulted. We do take some credit for putting them on the path toward their success, but they proved they could do it on their own, and I applaud their achievements.

Chapter Fourteen

Accidental Death and Other Mayhem

Anthony was a hard-working guy. He augmented his salary as a maintenance man at the Playboy Club in Vernon, New Jersey, by digging graves for a local cemetery. In May 1979, Anthony and his wife were living in a modest two-story frame home in Ogdensburg, New Jersey. A propane gas explosion at the home took his life and was the subject of our investigation. The insurance company that assigned us this case wanted a full workup, explaining that the insured was Littell Gas Service based in Sparta, New Jersey. It was no secret that then State Senator Robert E. Littell was the owner of the gas company and presented as a "target defendant" in practical terms.

Preliminary facts of the case were that Littell's delivery driver had filled the outside propane tank earlier that day, and somehow when Anthony came home and went downstairs, there was an explosion. Anthony was taken to the Allentown Sacred Heart burn unit, where he lingered in extreme pain for about thirty days before dying.

After picking up the police and fire reports, Linda and I went to the scene of the explosion. The basement of the home was nothing more than a dirt dugout approximately eight feet square. There was just room for the propane heater opposite the bottom of the steps leading into the area. On the left side we saw some of Anthony's skin still stuck to the stones that kept the dirt from caving in. It was not a pretty sight.

First, we made sure that the propane tank valve on the outside was shut off, then carefully inspected the heating unit. Nothing seemed out of the ordinary until I began working the Honeywell switch near the base. To initiate the gas flow, one had to push the small red plastic switch and turn it to the right where it should stay. Half the time, however, the switch would not stay in that position and would return to a full-on mode. It looked to me that there was something wrong with the switch and maybe this was the cause of this accident.

Further, the only light source was a light bulb and chain hanging from a wire and socket that swung back and forth when it knocked against my head in this confined space. Recalling a fire investigation course I took at Raritan Valley College several years before, I wondered: If the basement was filling with propane when Anthony pulled the chain, could that have been the ignition source? Propane has some peculiar qualities: First, it is heavier than air and its discharge will result in a heavier concentration collecting at the lowest level; as the gas builds up, the thinner concentration will be at the top. Next, the ignition point for propane is in neither the heavy nor the light concentration but is somewhere in between. In other words, too heavy or too light a concentration and it will not ignite, but just the right concentration of propane can ignite with the slightest spark. Surely, a light switch could supply that spark.

I needed to confirm my theory with the experts. After getting approval from the insurance carrier, I found a company that had the appropriate expertise. I revisited the scene with two engineers who systematically inspected everything, including the Honeywell plastic switch. A small outcropping on the plastic switch was meant to serve as a revolution stopper, but it had worn down. The mechanical engineer said it was a poor design and should have been metal. He was sure he could testify that the Honeywell switch was the cause of the propane gas leaking into the cellar. The other expert, a chemical engineer, confirmed my theory that the buildup of propane was ignited by the light switch in the pull chain, causing the explosion.

It didn't help Littell's case that its driver failed to restart the basement heater after doing the refill. Protocol suggested he should have done that, but Anthony's wife had told him not to worry. "Tony will be home soon and he can do that," she said. Little did they know at the time, because of the faulty switch, the propane was building up in the cellar. Anthony unknowingly pulled on the light chain and "whooosh!" The explosion, contained by the dirt walls, flashed and blew itself out, but poor Anthony took its brunt.

In the end, our investigation resulted in Honeywell sharing the liability and most of the financial burden of the lawsuit. Littell, our client, was wrong but so was Honeywell. Often in civil matters, the purpose of an investigation is to identify co-defendants to lessen the burden of a settlement or judgment for a client. That is what happened in this case.

Mass Murder in Hackettstown

As one might expect, an investigation agency is usually hired because there is a need for fact gathering that goes beyond the capability of the client. The rationale is the same when you hire a lawyer, doctor, or plumber. Sometimes you have to turn the job over to the expert. Our expertise arose from years of investigating civil, criminal, and corporate matters, but we are people, too, and some cases leave long-lasting impressions. The Hackettstown case was one of them.

In August 1977, Emile Pierre Benoist, a twenty-year-old ex-marine and the son of a prominent local politician, went on a killing rampage in Hackettstown, New Jersey. Late on a Friday afternoon, he fired his Ruger sniper rifle from a concealed position along a jogging path, leaving six dead and several others wounded. Later that night, the New Jersey State Police helicopter turned its spotlight on him in a cornfield, and Benoist, realizing his situation, turned the rifle on himself, thus ending the immediate ordeal.

The civil suits that followed, however, kept Hackettstown's wound open. Family members of the deceased sued the Town of Hackettstown and its police department for failing to recognize Benoist's deranged mental state and not taking action to prevent this horrific event. True, Benoist was an odd character. He said and did things that marked him as strange, but surely no one could have predicted that he would become a mass murderer. He had never been arrested or even taken into custody for any reason. The civil suits were considered a stretch by most legal minds. Nevertheless, the matter had to be defended, and you never know what a jury will do. Of course, the local police, state police, and the Warren County Prosecutor's Office conducted their investigation on the criminal side, and we had nothing to do with that. The insurance company with the policy on the Town of Hackettstown and hired us to provide evidence to help defend the civil case against the town.

One element of our assignment was to interview and take statements from every Hackettstown police officer to determine whether or not the officer had ever come into contact with Benoist. In working that investigation, my past police life was helpful. The Hackettstown officers started off cooperating with me rather than feeling they were being second-guessed by some insurance claims representative.

The insurance company executives saw no liability and would not yield any ground. How could the police possibly predict that this young man's sometimes bizarre behavior made him a serious danger to the community? Further, under our system of laws, you cannot take someone off the street just for being odd. Indeed, he didn't even have a past criminal record. Yet, this case was getting a lot of publicity, and sympathy for the surviving family members and was justifiably a serious factor. I had to come up with something that would get the insurance company officials to see just how vulnerable they were. I had to swing their hearts and minds. Often, it is not enough to be right; you need to look reality in the eye and take in the practical side of things, as well.

The decision makers needed to see and feel the shock and loss of life in real-people terms, not from within the safety of their offices and the cold, impersonal pieces of paper in the claims file. The autopsy color photos helped accomplish this. They were graphic and had a heavy impact at the insurance company. Those photographs showed bodies on the coroner's table. Their lifeless faces and opened abdomens said it all.

The lawyers ultimately reached some settlements, and the civil suits were dismissed. That was an emotionally charged case that has stuck with us over the years.

People who shuffle paper in offices day after day tend to lose sight of life's realities. There seems to be a disconnect between an insurance claim file or a lawyer's legal file and the impact that hardship has on people. I always tell law firm clients that there's more to know about almost every case by getting out on the street, as opposed to depending on what they have in their files. I admire the trial lawyer who goes out to the scene with me during an investigation. He or she is getting a better feel for the case by appreciating the nuances and variations that crop up in the real world. Later, when they are in negotiations, depositions, or trial, they are better equipped to do well for their client.

"Daddy, I Feel a Tingling . . ."

John A. was a history teacher in a Middlesex county high school. It was a Saturday in early spring, and he needed to clean his above-ground swimming pool. Over the winter, leaves and debris had collected in the pool along with about a foot of water. John decided he could clean out the leaves more efficiently by using a wet/dry vacuum, so he tied the tank part to the inside rim of the pool, while he and his ten-year-old daughter waded in the pool sucking up the leaves with the hose portion. The vacuum was hooked up to an extension cord plugged into the outside outlet on the house. That extension cord was also used to hold up the tank. In a very short time, the vacuum's five-gallon tank filled with water and its sixty-some pounds caused it to fall into the water. At that point, his daughter said, "Daddy, I feel a tingling!"

Realizing his mistake, John lifted his daughter by the waist and threw her up and over the rim of the pool. He told her to unplug the vacuum. Unfortunately, the daughter unplugged a radio sharing the double plug instead of the vacuum's extension cord. John, believing it was now safe, gripped the inside ladder intending to climb up and out. He was electrocuted and dead in seconds.

Our client, the manufacturer of the wet/dry vacuum, was not held responsible because the vacuum was used improperly and not as intended. John should never have used an electrical appliance so close to the water, exposing both him and his daughter to such danger. Sad case, but there has to be liability for a lawsuit to prevail.

TRESPASSING AND PARALYSIS

Another tragic case took place in rural Harmony Township, New Jersey, when a young man dove head first into the pond at the bottom of a quarry. From a height more than forty feet, he missed the deep water and landed headfirst in eighteen inches of water. He survived but was paralyzed for life.

Again, the defendant quarry owner was held faultless because he had erected a fence and posted signs all around the quarry area warning of its danger and to "Keep Out." Of course, that doesn't stop adventurous teens. They entered through a hole in the fence and went swimming on hot summer days in spite of continuous efforts by the owner to keep them out.

I also found multiple entries on the police blotter where the owner complained about trespassing. To show the remoteness of the quarry, I went up with a friend in his small plane and videotaped the surrounding area. The quarry was more than one thousand feet from the nearest road, yet the kids went swimming there anyway. Unfortunately, many of our accident cases were the result of foolish decisions by the injured party.

FIREWORKS

A young teenager lost all the fingers on his right hand and three on his left when a firecracker he was modifying in his family basement exploded. I met with him and his mother to discuss this homeowner claim. The boy's attorney came up with a novel theory. He alleged that the boy's own parents negligently allowed him to conduct experiments in the basement without supervision and filed a lawsuit against the parents. What moved me most was the comment made by his mother: "Until his prosthesis arrives, I have to wipe him like when he was a baby each time he goes to the bathroom. He can't even unzip his fly to urinate."

Eventually, a settlement was reached. Although the insurance carrier thought it could prevail on its legal merits, the case would have engendered a great deal of sympathy for the boy, and settling was the better part of valor.

Chapter Fifteen

Murder Cases

In the law-enforcement world, homicide investigations are definitely considered the "sexiest." Murder cases get front-page treatment by the press and grab public interest to the max. More than any other crimes, books are written and television shows are spawned about homicides and those who commit them. Defense lawyers love a good murder case. But it's not just defense counsel basking in the limelight during a murder trial. Many a prosecutor has advanced his or her political career thanks to the homicide launching pad.

Nevertheless, somehow the system works. With everyone innocent until proven guilty beyond a reasonable doubt, the burden is firmly on the prosecution to prove its case. The defense doesn't have to solve the case by proving someone else did the dirty deed. No, the defense just has to raise reasonable doubt that their guy did it. Alternative theories, police mistakes, discrediting witnesses, and legal technicalities are all fodder for defense counsel. The prosecution may have the benefit of investing lots of time and money into proving its case, while the defense, in contrast, often runs its case on a shoestring. Nevertheless, the system is weighted on the side of the defense, considering all they have to do is raise reasonable doubt.

I have worked for the defense on a half-dozen murder cases as a private investigator. Four resulted in convictions, and I lost no sleep over "losing" those cases. I did my job and gave the defense attorney what was needed in each case. That they did not prevail speaks to proficient police investigations and prosecution. Those cases were losers from the start. But the other two cases were not as clear-cut. One may have been a miscarriage of justice, and I will get to that one later. Then there was the Elizabeth O'Connor murder case. What had been a cold case after eight years of inactivity became a crusade by two detectives to convict our client on the basis of old eyewitness testimony and no forensics at all.

MURDER AT THE MALL

In the summer of 1980, attorney Ernie Duh summoned me to his office to tell me he had a client accused of a murder that occurred eight years earlier. He had a stack of police reports for me to review, which took me the better part of the afternoon. Close to five p.m., he came back into the conference room and said, "So, what do you think? Stinks, doesn't it?"

It did. Here's what happened. Elizabeth O'Connor lived with her family in rural Pohatcong Township, New

Jersey. One Saturday morning in 1972, she drove the family camper to the Hillcrest Mall in Phillipsburg, New Jersey, alone, parked, and went shopping for some last-minute items for the family's upcoming getaway. This mall was not a high-crime area; it was a relatively safe location with local residents coming and going.

Her shopping done, O'Connor got back to her vehicle. She no sooner got into the driver's seat then she was grabbed from behind and pulled into the rear of the camper. One of her flip-flops was later found under the brake pedal. What actually took place is not clear, as the police report was speculative. What is known is that about ten minutes later, O'Connor was found almost two miles away on the roadway, her head severely injured in a fall from the moving camper. No one knows if she jumped or was thrown from the camper. She never regained consciousness to describe her attacker or attackers.

Strangely, the camper was returned to the Hillcrest Mall shortly afterward. The local police sent an officer to secure the van, but when rain threatened, he got behind the wheel and drove it to headquarters, thus destroying any fingerprints that might have been found on the steering wheel. In fact, no fingerprints were found anywhere in the camper other than those of Elizabeth and her family.

The local police were not up to investigating a difficult murder case like this, so the New Jersey State Police became involved. The trooper detectives set up a table in front of the mall and made inquiries in the hope of finding anyone who might have seen anything that

Saturday morning. Three witnesses came forward. One was an unmarried mother on welfare. The other two were a young couple who had driven into the mall parking lot just as the camper careened out onto the roadway. The driver said he had to swerve to avoid being hit by the camper. All three witnesses described the driver as a young white man in his twenties with dark hair and olive complexion. They were shown some photos of convicted local criminals, but no identification was made at that time. It is no surprise that eventually the case went cold. Any homicide detective will tell you random killings are the most difficult to solve. With no relationship to the victim, there is no thread to follow in terms of motive— and in this case, no forensics, as well.

Time passed with no new leads. Then eight years later a career criminal in Rahway Prison said he had some information about a murder case near Phillipsburg where a woman was thrown from a camper. He wanted to make a deal for early parole. Two New Jersey State Police detectives were assigned to go to the prison and interview the convict. He gave them the name of the person he believed was responsible for Elizabeth O'Connor's death. The detectives checked it out and determined that the man named by the convict was in prison at the time of the murder and thus could not have been the perpetrator.

Before going to the prison for the interview, however, the two detectives reviewed this cold-case file. While interviewing the convict did not produce a positive result for the detectives, the review of the file got them fired up about the case. There's nothing like the possibility of solving a cold case that energizes police detectives. Doing so means you must be smarter and more resourceful than those who preceded you.

They zeroed in on Robert Piperato, a resident of Easton, Pennsylvania, just over the Delaware River from Phillipsburg. He was the right age and fit the description. He had been interviewed by police eight years prior as a possible person of interest, and he had a criminal record for petty theft. The detectives went back to the three witnesses who, now after eight years, were somehow able to identify Piperato as the driver of the camper leaving the mall in a hurry.

Attorney Duh was right. It smelled. First, the passage of eight years between the act and the identification of the driver made that identification suspect (witness testimony is considered somewhat unreliable, anyway). Further, the identifications were made from a photo lineup, called a show-up. These are black-and-white police photographs taken at the time those in the show-up were previously arrested. Then you have the young driver suddenly swerving to avoid hitting the camper. Under the threat of a possible auto accident, how could he have made a reliable observation of the camper driver?

Based solely on these three witness statements, however, Piperato was arrested and charged with Elizabeth O'Connor's murder. Again, no forensics—just these three witnesses.

Duh wanted me to interview the witnesses and

find out what photographs they were shown by the detectives. First I interviewed the single mother, who lived in a dilapidated two-story home in a rural area of Warren County, New Jersey. The steep steps leading up to the front porch were littered with children's toys and nondescript items abandoned over time. The woman met me at the front door, obviously reluctant to discuss the case. She allowed me past the threshold and into her house, where we sat at the kitchen table surrounded by relatives of the junk on the sidewalk.

"So, if I already talked to the cops, why are you here? I picked out the guy I saw in the camper—the one who killed that lady." I asked her to go over the details of her meeting with the detectives, but she wasn't having any of it. "I don't see how that has anything to do with anything. They showed me pictures and I picked the guy out. That's it."

I reached into my briefcase and pulled out a stack of about one hundred arrest photographs that Duh had requested from the prosecutor's office. Piperato's photo was among them. Duh admitted, "This is one helluva chance, but we have to take it."

"Please look these over and tell me if you see the driver of the camper from these photos. Frankly, I don't know if he is in here or not, but you might be able to tell."

Glaring at me, her head tilted and lips pursed, she said, "I'll look, but this isn't fair. The detectives only showed me eight or ten pictures and said the guy they thought was the killer was one of them."

Unbelievable! The detectives actually showed the

witness photographs after advising her that their suspect was one of them. That put pressure on the witness to come up with the "right" choice.

The correct verbiage is, "Do you see the man who drove the camper among these photographs?" There can be nothing in the questioning of a witness during a lineup or a show-up that suggests the one the police suspect is actually in one of the photographs. After going through the stack, the witness said, "I don't think he's in here. You are trying to trick me. You should leave now."

Later that day at Duh's office, we thought we were on the right track. Going after the identifications was really our only defense. We knew there was a lot of pressure by the state police on Howard McGinn, the Warren County prosecutor, but we also knew him to be a fair and honest guy. We needed more.

The following week Duh left a message on my voicemail: "Dave, that witness you talked to last week complained to Howard's office that you tried to confuse her with all those photographs. She wants to stand by her original identification with the detectives. Call me."

Duh suggested that I send another private investigator to re-interview the witness. Even though he and McGinn knew I wouldn't tamper with a witness, which is a crime, we still had to deal with the situation. I called Bruce Snyder in Lansdale, Pennsylvania. He is the best investigator I ever met and I trusted him. He interviewed the witness and ended up with the same results as I did.

I agreed with Snyder that this woman would make a lousy witness for the prosecution and that her prime motivation was getting her fifteen minutes of fame. That's a problem with some witnesses. While most folks would rather not get involved, some relish the attention.

We then focused on the other two witnesses. The young man (let's call him Tom) said he and his girlfriend broke up and she moved to the Orlando area. He told us he was unsure of his identification and had just wanted to cooperate with the police investigators. Duh felt he could easily neutralize him on the witness stand.

The ex-girlfriend (let's call her Nancy) was another matter. I tracked her down and spoke with her on the telephone. She was pretty sure of her identification of Piperato. "Hey, the cops showed me the pictures and I saw the guy driving the camper right away. No problem."

As the trial date grew near, Duh sent me to Orlando to talk to Nancy, who lived in a small cinder block and stucco ranch-style cottage. Her overly tweezed eyebrows, pierced ears, and bright red lip gloss gave her a tough appearance—no doubt, intended.

When I asked her about the police show-up of the photographs, her version was slightly different from what she told me on the phone. "The cops showed me a bunch of photos and I picked the guy out. It was a long time ago, but I told them he was *the one that looked most like the guy* me and Tom saw driving the camper that day. Poor lady. Did she have any kids?"

I took her statement, including the wording we

needed to show that this was not a positive identification but a tentative "look-alike" observation on her part. She agreed to return to New Jersey if needed for trial and asked several times about Tom, the old boyfriend. "He was a sweet guy. I never shoulda busted up with him. Will I see him when I get back there?"

Duh took Nancy's statement to the prosecutor's office and met with McGinn. Considering the first witness's comments on how the state police introduced the show-up to her, Tom's acquiescence, and Nancy's signed statement, we thought sure the prosecutor would drop the case. Unfortunately, the prosecutor didn't feel he had enough to go against the state police, so we headed off to trial.

Nancy was brought in from Orlando, and Linda and I went to meet her at Newark Airport. She appeared from the Jetway wearing a bright red blouse, yellow neckerchief, and tight rhinestone-studded black pants tucked into white cowgirl boots. With her hands on her hips and one knee turned in, she said, "Wait till he gets a look at me!" For sure, Nancy was more interested in impressing former boyfriend, Tom, than the jury.

The morning of the trial, Duh and I went back and forth between confidence and anxiety as we discussed our chances. Finally, Duh said, "Let's give Howard one more chance. I have an idea."

Duh and McGinn were in the latter's office for about ten minutes. When they came out, Duh shot me a wink and a head shake that said, "Shhhh, don't say anything!"

We had not yet chosen a jury and the courtroom was beginning to fill up with onlookers, the press, and a few courthouse employees. Murder trials do attract attention.

I was sitting in the rear of the courtroom when Duh and McGinn came out of the door to the judge's chambers with Nancy and Tom. She giggled self-consciously, while Tom looked like he would rather be anywhere else. All stood looking out at the assembled crowd. Neither the defendant's nor prosecutor's tables were occupied, so no obvious defendant stood out. I could barely hear her, but Nancy said, "That's him . . . second row, one, two, three . . . yeah, third from the right." She pointed into the crowd while turning to Tom. He, acquiescent as always, nodded his head in agreement. They had identified an insurance salesman from Hackettstown, not our client who was seated several rows back.

Duh smiled; McGinn frowned. Duh later explained, "I told Howard that once my client is seated at the defense table, what witness is going to doubt the identity of the defendant? Won't the pressure be on them to point to him? What if they're wrong? Let's see if she can identify him without the suggestion."

Prosecutor McGinn and Duh met with the judge and the case against Bob Piperato was dismissed without prejudice. That means, since the trial had not started, should the prosecution come up with any new evidence, double jeopardy would not attach and the case against Piperato could be reopened.

Piperato walked. The prosecution's case was weak.

It relied on three eyewitnesses making the briefest of observations under stressful conditions. Worse, the identifications were made more than eight years after the fact. With no forensics to back up the witnesses, the case was a sham.

Now let's go back to that day at the Hillcrest Mall when Elizabeth O'Connor returned to her camper after shopping. She was grabbed from behind, and the camper took off, careening out of the mall with O'Connor in the back.

We have to consider what would be a natural course of events. First, is it reasonable for one person to grab the victim and pull her to the back and then take off with her alone and loose back there? It is more likely that there were two involved in this kidnapping and unintended murder. I believe that the two were surprised by O'Connor's return as they were going through the camper looking for things to steal. They panicked, realizing if they simply ran from the van in the mall parking lot, then O'Connor would likely yell and notify the police. Instead, they took off in the camper with her.

The police investigation never even considered there was more than one perpetrator, yet O'Connor didn't fall from the camper until she was nearly two miles from the mall. There was likely a struggle going on in the back as the camper was driven away. Her exit from the camper was probably not part of the plan, either.

Let's look at the question of why the camper was returned to the mall. Although never discussed openly, it seems obvious that the perpetrators had their own car back in the lot and needed to return to complete their getaway. Back then there were no security cameras monitoring the parking lots, so they were home free once they switched to their own vehicle. The New Jersey State Police detectives, however, continued to believe that the perpetrator acted alone and that he was Bob Piperato.

Piperato was a loner. He did not hang out with a group; his minor previous arrest record did not involve any cohorts. I met with Piperato and his young wife in an Easton diner when I first took this case on. I can't say that I believed he was innocent or guilty of this crime. I can say that when I met with him, he was a calm and deliberate individual who had a job. He was in his mid-twenties and looked me straight in the eye and said, "Mr. Watts, I've made a lot of mistakes in my life, but that's all in the past. I never hurt anyone, and I was not involved in stealing that camper and hurting that lady."

I've been lied to and fooled by the best, so Piperato's denial on its own didn't convince me. After working on the case, however, I believed this was an instance where two overzealous detectives tried to crack a cold case without enough evidence to reach trial. Thanks to the integrity of Prosecutor McGinn and the savvy representation of attorney Duh, the trial ended before it began. It might have been an uphill battle, but I still think we would have discredited the witness testimony if, indeed, this case had gone to trial. But who knows? Juries do strange things sometimes.

Elizabeth O'Connor's murder is unsolved to this day, with no justice for her or her family. Had the local patrolman not driven the camper to headquarters and destroyed any possible fingerprint evidence on the steering wheel, this case might have taken a completely different turn. We'll never know.

Several years later, we took on another murder defense case that still has me hanging in midair.

Guilty as Hell or a Father's Love?

Donald Moringiello, a sixty-four-year-old retired aeronautical engineer, lived with his wife, Hattie "Fern" Bergeler, in their million-dollar waterfront estate home on Estero Island, Florida. Their low-slung ranch home had a screened pool and a newly installed upper floor toward the rear overlooking their dock on Estero Bay. That dock would play a major role in this case. Both previously divorced, the couple met while employed at Pratt and Whitney in West Palm Beach.

Once retired, the couple moved to Fort Myers Beach on Estero Island and bought the Randy Lane home. They owned a condo in Fort Myers, as well. Life was good. The couple fit in well with the neighbors and became well known for their wine and cheese parties.

There was a wrinkle, however. Donald had a son, Doug, who did not get along with Fern. Doug was over six feet tall and weighed 250 pounds. He ran with a rough crowd, all with drug habits. More on Doug later.

On July 18, 2002, Fern Bergeler's body was found face down in eighteen inches of water by three fishermen just a quarter mile south of the Moringiello dock and about fifty feet from the shoreline. The body was wrapped in a white king-sized bed sheet and tied to several cinderblocks. She had been in the warm water of the bay for several days, which meant a great deal of sea life predation to the body had occurred. The autopsy report indicated the victim had been shot four times in the chest with a small-caliber gun.

Initially, the police were unable to identify the fifty-seven-year-old retiree because she was never reported missing by her husband. Fliers were distributed in the area, with a description of the garden clothes worn by the victim in an attempt to identify her. Subsequently, Bergeler's niece in Alabama called the Lee County Sheriff's Office to report her aunt missing. This led to the body being identified as Bergeler's.

Moringiello's answer to the question of why he hadn't reported his wife missing was that they had an argument and she walked out. He then took a two-week vacation in New England. When he returned home and saw that his wife wasn't there, he called her niece in Alabama, who then called the sheriff. That niece had never approved of Moringiello and his marriage to her aunt, so when she made the call to police, she conveyed her fear that he had done away with Bergeler. She also portrayed Moringiello's attitude during his call to her as suspicious.

Police were not happy with Moringiello's answers,

and a search of the Moringiello home produced rope, cinderblocks, and linens that appeared to match those evidential items found on the body. The detectives also found blood in the hallway leading to the bathroom, just off the master bedroom. In fact, the flooring in the bathroom had been recently changed and once torn up, showed traces of blood. Not only that, police divers actually found the murder weapon, a .32-caliber pistol, in the water off the dock. That gun was registered to Donald Moringiello.

It didn't look good for Moringiello. He steadfastly denied any involvement in his wife's disappearance or death; yet his responses to police questions were ambiguous and pointed to him as the killer. He was arrested and charged with second-degree murder. Over a two-year period, he went to trial twice. The first trial ended with a hung jury, but he was convicted on the second go-round.

At left, Defendant Donald Moringiello on date of his arrest, August 14, 2002. (Lee County Sheriff's public website) Convicted at second trial, he was booked in at South Florida Reception Center (right) on November 3, 2005. (Florida Department of Corrections public website.)

Rear view from Estero Bay of Moringiello's million dollar waterfront home. (Lee County Sheriff's Office crime scene photo)

At the outset, however, attorney Wilbur Smith of Fort Myers called me and said he and his partner, Joe Viacava, would be representing Moringiello on the murder charge. Smith is what one might call a "good ole boy." He wears alligator boots and speaks with a Southern twang. Upon entry to the Wilbur Smith law firm, the first thing you see is a stuffed fourteen-foot alligator mounted on a large table off to the left. Smith will explain that he shot the beast one night while gator hunting. The former mayor of Fort Myers, he is a soft-spoken gentleman who is well respected by bench and bar throughout Southwest Florida. In contrast, Viacava, the younger of the two, is a New York City transplant who comes across as arrogant and pushy. Hey, he's from New Yawk! I worked many cases for the firm, and found both Smith and Viacava to be excellent lawyers who complemented each other well in the courtroom.

At this time, I had on staff a retired Miami homicide detective, George Cavada. Cavada and I, accompanied by attorney Viacava, sat down with Moringiello in jail to interview him. He denied killing his wife but could not give a plausible accounting of his whereabouts between the time the body was found and when it was finally identified almost a month later. His vague answers bothered me. Here we had an educated aeronautical engineer who surely knew his responses were not satisfactory, yet he continued down that route. There were large gaps in the timeline we put together and he just shrugged.

Also, the facts of the case were puzzling. Why would

a smart guy like Moringiello, after shooting his wife to death, wrap her up in household linens, truss her up using the family's rope and cinderblocks, and chuck her off the back dock? Why would he then throw the murder weapon off the dock right there in the back yard? He had a small boat at the dock and could easily have taken the body into the Gulf of Mexico under the cover of darkness. Had he done that, assuming he was the shooter, the body and gun would likely never have been found. It just didn't make sense.

Part of our participation in the case involved interviewing neighbors and going through the Moringiello house to see if there was anything the detectives missed or, indeed, failed to add to their report that might help the defense. We went up and down the adjoining streets interviewing just about every neighbor we could find. All liked the Moringiellos. Many socialized with them, and none could envision Moringiello killing his wife.

We got the key to the house from the law firm, and Cavada and I went over to Fort Myers Beach to take a look. When we got there, we saw Moringiello's son, Doug, and his girlfriend standing waist deep in the swimming pool. Doug just stared at us as we explained we were from the law firm and would be looking around inside. He barely nodded his head and went back to paying attention to his girlfriend. *That's weird,* I thought. *Wouldn't you think the son could have come up from the pool and asked about progress on his father's case?* But not a word—just a blank stare.

Because the police report indicated two unwashed wine glasses had been found on the counter in the Moringiello's condo in Fort Myers, Cavada and I also visited there. Police speculation about the wine glasses centered on the possibility that Bergeler might have been having an extramarital affair, but no fingerprints could be obtained, leaving that theory dangling in outer space.

Outside we saw Doug's van parked in the lot. We took a close look and found that all the windows were blocked. We knew from his father that Doug had a drug habit. Cavada and I both believed Doug's demeanor was odd and that the van could contain forensics that might help our case.

I called Viacava and asked if there was a way we could get a look inside Doug's van with a forensics expert. I thought that Moringiello may have been covering up for his son. The fact that Fern's own minivan was inexplicably found on Florida's East Coast also brought me back to Doug and his friends. But Viacava thought our theory was "too farfetched," and Doug's van escaped scrutiny.

Between the first and second trials, Doug died of an overdose of heroin. Now Smith and Viacava did their best to portray Doug as the alternative perpetrator, but the prosecutor did a much better job this second time and Moringiello was convicted. I wish we could have gotten into Doug's van when we first spotted it.

There was much more to the case than you have read here, as there always is in murder cases. Moringiello certainly could have killed his wife; yet Doug's heroin addiction and his antipathy toward Bergeler is just as firm a reason for him to have done it.

To me the most compelling aspect of this theory is the blundering disposal of the body. This whole scenario fits much better with Doug, the son, as the killer. It also makes sense that Moringiello could have been covering up for his son, whom he admitted he had let down over the years.

As I write this, Don Moringiello is incarcerated for life in a Florida prison—either an innocent man or a heartless killer. We will likely never know.

Chapter Sixteen

Trials and Other Tribulations

Testimony at trial or in depositions is the ultimate test of an investigator's work. Our job is done, the evidence obtained and preserved, the report submitted, and our bill paid, so what else could there be? But as the saying goes, "The opera ain't over till the fat lady sings."

Court testimony is opera-like in many respects. There is a story line to which the players adhere. In this large room, there is tension in the air. The score is conducted by a person dressed in black waving a small piece of wood at the front of the stage. There are emotional outbursts, periodic intermissions, and, ultimately, a winner and a loser. When it's over, the audience renders its appreciation with vocal approval or otherwise. See the formality of the courtroom and the grandiose nature of the opera house? See the judge in robes with a gavel and the musical conductor with a baton? See the jury ensconced in its special section and the opera box seats full of enraptured onlookers? See the lawyers and the principal actors emoting their best? See the story or testimony building to a crescendo when the jury renders its verdict and the opera house erupts in applause?

Trial is the showplace of the case. Of course, many legal battles don't go to trial. Facts come out through discovery, both sides weigh their positions, negotiations produce accommodations, and settlements are reached. When neither side will budge, however, the stage is set, the curtain goes up, and "the fat lady sings."

I have testified in hundreds of the more than six thousand investigations we handled in more than thirty-eight years in business. As a fact witness, I must not show any bias toward one side or other, but when I am called to step up there, everyone knows whose side I am on. I must be respectful at all times, but sometimes it's tough to give a "yes" or "no" to those damned-if you-do, damned-if-you-don't kinds of questions that lawyers pose. It is up to my client's attorney to smooth over or blunt any points scored by opposing counsel in re-cross examination, if necessary. Not my job. My job on the witness stand is to tell it like it is and leave it at that. Of all those cases where I testified, however, one stands out as special. It was the one time I spoke up, and rightfully so.

" . . . And Sho' Nuff, the Roof Caved In!"

David Jackson was claims manager at Hanover Insurance Company's office in Piscataway, New Jersey. We had been working insurance defense cases for Jackson and his staff for about a year when he called.

"David, we have a doozy for you," he said. "We are in trial in New York County (that's Manhattan), and it's getting wilder by the minute. Please stop in to discuss."

Later that day at his office, Jackson explained that a few years earlier the roof of Alexander's warehouse on Long Island had caved in, and the owners, the Rodolitz brothers, had submitted a claim for several million dollars. Over the course of the claim, Hanover Insurance sent structural engineers to inspect the site. The engineering report placed blame for the collapse on the new and much heavier air conditioning units that were installed not long before the collapse. The report said, "The roof simply was not designed to carry that heavy a load." Ergo, the defense theory was that damage resulting from the roof collapse was caused by the insured's failure to install the proper units. In other words, it was their own fault and the insurance policy had an exclusion covering just such a circumstance.

Naturally, the engineering report supplied by the Rodolitz brothers did not agree and their experts submitted a different theory. As is often the case where expert testimony is involved, one side offsets the other, making it all the more difficult to arrive at a verdict. In this case, there was no jury, just the judge hearing the matter. The trial had been going on for several days, and the wrangling among attorneys had pissed off the judge. The air in the courtroom was tense with one outburst after another. To add more drama to this case, during a settlement conference before the trial began, one of the Rodolitz boys threatened to throw Jackson out of a window if Hanover Insurance didn't pay up.

In a deposition, Hanover's counsel asked one of the Rodolitz brothers, "You had a maintenance man, didn't you?"

Rodolitz answered, "Yes, we did. He had a stroke a while ago and doesn't work for us anymore. I think he's dead."

Inasmuch as the Rodolitz brothers had a reputation for being less than forthcoming, Jackson assigned us the task of finding the maintenance man and either interviewing him or confirming his death. "Find out what happened to the maintenance man. If he is still alive, talk to him. See what he knows about that roof, David."

It took the better part of a day, but I located the maintenance man's apartment in a rough neighborhood in Garden City, Long Island. Brown lived on the third floor of a project building, and I admit I approached his door with some anxiety. I rang the doorbell.

"Are you the same Warren Brown who used to work at Alexander's warehouse?" I asked.

"Yes, that's me. Who are you?"

I showed him my New York State P.I. identification and he let me in. It was a small one-bedroom apartment but very well kept. Brown led me to his kitchen table, indicating I should have a seat. I then noticed a young woman seated nearby on a sofa, who introduced herself as Brown's daughter. Brown was a slightly built black man in his sixties, soft-spoken, and old-school respectful.

I got right to the point. "Mr. Brown, since you were the maintenance man, do you have any idea why that roof collapsed?"

"I told 'em. I told 'em. Those new air conditioners was too heavy. I used to go out on the roof to seal up some little leaks. I can tell you, if I went out in the middle and just jumped up and down a little bit, the whole roof went up and down, too. I was scared to go out there. I told Mr. Rod 'bout that, and sho' nuff, the roof caved in."

Brown said he had a stroke about six months earlier but was doing much better now. We made some small talk, and then I asked, "Do you mind if I take a report down about this? I just want my bosses to know I got it right from you."

Glancing over toward his daughter for support, he said, "No problem, I guess." She signaled her approval with a slight nod of the head.

I had a portable typewriter with me, so I began taking down Brown's personal information to identify the witness, then launched into the good stuff. His statement completely discredited the Rodolitz brothers' version of the roof collapse.

When we reached the end where I type, "I have read this two-page typewritten statement and it is the truth to the best of my knowledge and belief," I paused. Just getting Brown's signature on this statement may not be enough. This trial was already contentious with lawyers screaming at each other and the judge acting like he just came off the set of television's *Law and Order*. I knew the statement was important evidence, but I also knew I would have to defend it in the highly charged atmosphere of the courtroom. *How can I show this statement was taken without any undue pressure on Mr. Brown?*

"Mr. Brown, do you mind if I turn this recorder on and read the statement back to you?" I read the statement, breaking it down into sections where I would periodically insert, "Is that right?" Each time Brown said, "Yup, that's just what happened." The tape whirred on, taking in every syllable.

Toward the end of the recording, I asked Brown about his stroke and he repeated that he felt much better now. I asked his daughter if her father understood everything we had done and she agreed. On the tape she identified herself as an elementary school teacher. It was very helpful that the daughter was supportive of the statement and the recording, but to be an educated schoolteacher was icing on the cake.

I called Jackson to give him the news and dropped off the statement the next morning. Jackson gave me a subpoena to be served on Brown that night. Back in Garden City, all the way from Cokesbury, I rang the doorbell, but this time got no immediate response. I feared that the Rodolitz boys found out about my meeting with Brown, and my thoughts drifted to images of his bloody body wrapped in a rug in the nearest landfill when a young and antagonistic male voice came from inside the apartment. "Go away. Ain't nobody here talking to you." I left the subpoena under the door shouting, "You are served!"

The next day I got a call from Jackson. He said, "Mr. Brown came into court but had to have help getting up onto the witness stand. All he could manage to say was, 'I . . . can't . . . talk.' David, he was playing the stroke thing to the hilt. What bullshit! Rodolitz's lawyer went ape claiming we were taking advantage of a sick old man. The judge isn't happy with us, either. It was an Academy Award performance. We need you in court tomorrow."

The next morning I was sworn in and settled into the witness chair. After fully identifying me, Hanover's attorney asked, "Mr. Watts, can you identify this as the statement you took from Mr. Brown?"

"Yes, that's it."

"Was this statement given voluntarily, and did Mr. Brown understand what he was signing?"

"Yes. Absolutely."

He then turned to the Rodolitz lawyer. "Your witness."

I have been cross-examined many times in my career. It's always because my testimony was damaging to the other side and opposing counsel needs to neutralize that testimony. My job is to give honest answers and not engage in any argumentative exchanges. But I knew I was in for a tough time here.

He looked at me scornfully and started with, "Let me see your identification."

I gave him my folder with my New York State

Private Investigator license. He looked at it for a moment, then looked up at the judge saying, "Your Honor, this suggests that Mr. Watts is a New York state employee. It has the state seal on it. Clearly, Your Honor, this is a case of misrepresentation. This private investigator tricked the witness into believing he was an official from the State of New York. I move to place this identification card and the folder into evidence. Further, I move to strike that fake statement and his entire testimony as false and prejudicial."

His Honor leaned forward and motioned a "give it here" with two fingers. The judge inspected my identification, while the attorney ranted on about improper investigative behavior and how the court could allow such abuse of one of its elderly citizens . . . blah, blah, blah.

The judge was not impressed, "This looks like proper identification to me. Here, give it back to the man and get on with your cross."

Undefeated, the lawyer came back at me. "Isn't it a fact that when you saw Mr. Brown, he was ill and unable to understand your intentions? You tricked him into signing this nonsense you call a statement?" He waved the statement around and then threw it down onto his table in disgust.

"No, sir," I calmly stated. "Mr. Brown understood every word of it. We had a pleasant conversation, and that statement fairly represents what he told me."

I glanced over at Jackson sitting with the Hanover

attorney. He was looking down, obviously suppressing a grin, with his lips tightly mashed together. The Hanover lawyer was gazing at the ceiling, his head turning away, no doubt stifling laughter. They were waiting for opposing counsel to give me the opening I needed to get the recording introduced into evidence.

"Fair, you say. Is it fair to take advantage of an old, sick man? Is it fair to come into this court and give false testimony? Is it fair to sell yourself to an insurance company like this? You disgust me. Obviously, Mr. Watts, given what we know, there's no way to resolve this, is there? No further questions of this witness, your honor." He sat down with smug confidence oozing.

Actually, the Rodolitz lawyer was doing a good job. He was following the old legal axiom: if you can't win on the facts, attack the witness.

Seeing that opening we were waiting for, I twisted to face the judge. "Your Honor, can I answer the last question?"

His Honor, a bit surprised, frowned and said, "What question?"

"He asked how we could resolve this. I think I can do that."

The judge sat back, perplexed. Peering over the top of his glasses, he inquired, "Just how do you propose to do that?" He snuck a quick sideways look over at Hanover's attorney, whose slightest nod suggested agreement.

"Your Honor, I not only took Mr. Brown's statement down on paper, I tape recorded it with his permission, as well. Mr. Brown agreed that to have a clear understanding of those facts, we should make this recording, too. You'll see what I mean, if you allow me to play it."

The Rodolitz lawyer shot out of his seat, but before he could say a word, the judge sat straight up in his chair and in a no-nonsense tone said, "Let's hear the tape." His left-handed brush-off gesture pushed opposing counsel back into his seat. The lawyer slumped a little lower than before, as the Rodolitz brother seated next to him grabbed his arm and whispered in his ear. At the same time, the court reporter disdainfully pushed back from his machine, shaking his head from side to side. He was not going to try to take down any garbled crap from a tape recorder.

I played the recording, attaching a small amplifier to the machine. It all came out clear as could be with Brown's words reverberating throughout the courtroom. It left no doubt that Brown gave his statement voluntarily. Indeed, it presented convincing supportive evidence that the roof of the Alexander warehouse was not sufficiently constructed to bear the weight of those new air conditioning units and that the Rodolitz brothers knew it. The opposition was thoroughly deflated.

The Rodolitz brothers lost. Hanover paid its original nominal offer to settle the claim, saving several million dollars. That case was, for me, the quintessential courtroom drama. No, it wasn't a juicy murder case or a mobster headliner, but it was the kind of case you never forget.

Insurance Company Motto: " Whenever the Going Gets Tough, Just Chicken Out!"

State Farm was for a time our biggest insurance client, and we always enjoyed our relationship with its claims professionals. Its Special Investigation Unit (SIU) sent us a case, however, that ended up threatening our business with the company. In this particular case the claimant, a middle-aged woman, was asserting that her injuries precluded any activity on her part—walking, lifting, bending, or concentrating on anything. Her claim allegations included constant back, neck, and shoulder pain. She said she used to be active in her community, played tennis, and enjoyed gardening, but now was relegated to watching television and taking trips to her doctors. Her attorney, an experienced plaintiff's lawyer known to State Farm as a tough negotiator, was inflating her claim at every turn. Her medical bills had reached $60,000 plus, and she was still being treated. Her attorney's demand was $500,000 to settle, which State Farm rejected.

The insurance company's defense counsel requested an independent medical examination (IME), which is the norm for this type of case. The examining doctor noted good muscle tone with no apparent atrophy. At the exam, the claimant stood up quickly from her chair unaided and though she affected a limp on the way in, she walked normally with no limp out in the parking lot, according to the doctor. Her case was almost two years old, yet her complaints centered on soft tissue injury. Nearly all muscle strains and sprains clear up in the first six months unless there is nerve damage or a fracture involved. The IME doctor opined, " . . . the plaintiff appears to be exaggerating her discomfort, which will likely abate as soon as she receives monetary compensation." Thus, our surveillance investigation was requested.

We gave the assignment to Ian Ressler, who came to our agency right out of college with a criminal justice degree. He worked hard, wrote clear and concise reports, and grew quickly into an excellent surveillance investigator taking rock-steady video. He was a tall, thin, gangly, and respectful young man who never cut corners in his work.

Ressler did his homework. He ran a check with the New Jersey Division of Motor Vehicles, checked the tax list to be sure the claimant had not moved, and researched our online restricted-access databases for anything else that might help identify the subject once he took to the field. He then set up a surveillance position a couple of blocks away, but within view of the front of the subject's house so he could monitor her driveway in case she drove off.

Time went by with no activity, so Ressler decided to make a pass by her house. The direction he drove from put him on the opposite side of the street from the claimant's house. As he came up, he saw activity inside the glassed-in front porch, so he came to a quick stop at the curb and jumped into the back of his minivan. Lifting his video camera and shooting through the van's side window, he captured the claimant moving heavy furniture around on the porch. The large porch windows afforded a clear and unobstructed view of the woman to anyone passing by.

Following his auto accident, he claimed total disability and could no longer work due to excruciating pain. We videotaped him painting an apartment complex. (Photo from author's investigation files)

She wore a neck brace and walked with a cane during a medical examination two days previous to our videotaping her running from a restaurant and jumping into a friend's car. (Photo from author's investigation files)

When Ressler returned to the office and proudly showed us his videotape, we all congratulated him and called it in to State Farm's SIU in Cherry Hill, New Jersey. They were equally thrilled with Ressler's video evidence.

Then came the trial, and everything changed. The plaintiff's attorney alleged that Ressler had violated one of New Jersey's stalking statutes and requested that the judge refer his actions to the prosecutor's office. State Farm's attorney strenuously disagreed and ably argued that the plaintiff's activity took place in plain sight, as anyone on the street could have seen what Ressler saw, and there certainly was no invasion of privacy. In an effort to give the plaintiff her day in court, the judge reluctantly acceded to opposing counsel and referred it to the prosecutor.

The prosecutor came back within twenty-four hours stating that no law was broken, citing the "in plain sight" doctrine. The trial continued. The jury saw the videotape and came back with a verdict granting the plaintiff only her medical damages of $68,500. By any measure, this was a complete win for State Farm, and its house counsel told me so as he congratulated us just outside the courtroom.

Present at the trial, however, was a *Newark Star Ledger* reporter who covered the trial on a daily basis and wrote a scathing condemnation of State Farm and our company because we allowed our investigator to photograph into someone's home with impunity. The article appeared on the bottom of the front page of the most widely read newspaper in New Jersey. It included an interview with Jimmy Mesis, president of the New

Jersey Private Detective Association, who agreed that private detectives should not photograph people within the confines of their homes. Mesis regularly worked for plaintiff lawyers, so his response could be expected. But in this case the plaintiff was on her porch in full view of anyone on the street with no expectation of privacy. The prosecutor agreed. The jury apparently did as well. They compensated the plaintiff only for her medical bills, not the $500,000 her attorney was demanding.

Once the newly appointed vice president of State Farm got wind of the newspaper article, he forbade the SIU investigators from using our company again. His rationale was that no matter how much money we saved the company, the *Star Ledger* article embarrassed State Farm and we were out. State Farm's house counsel wrote me a nice letter stating he believed we did a great job on the case; but he was, after all, an employee of State Farm and he was not about to take on a vice president. Fortunately, that vice president had no sway over the regular State Farm claims department, so we continued to work for the company, just not for the special investigation unit.

That State Farm executive missed an opportunity. He could have issued a press release stating that State Farm will fight fraud wherever it can and this case is a perfect example of how the system works to protect the citizens and policyholders of New Jersey against insurance fraud and abuse. He could have cited the wisdom of his claims staff in noticing the flags of an overstated claim and then taking appropriate action. He could have applauded the jury's verdict refusing to reward the plaintiff for pain and suffering that was demonstrated to be fraudulent. But, no, the typical corporate coward, he chickened out.

"Follow That Garbage Truck!"

Our first case with State Farm had been assigned by Beth Ward, a tough-talking woman who didn't pull any punches. She was dissatisfied with another investigation firm that had been unable to get the goods on a young man Ward knew was a phony claimant.

"So, you come well recommended," she said to me, "but can you take this on right away? The trial is not far off, and discovery time is running out."

The opportunity to work for State Farm was all I needed to jump on this one. I assigned Joe Canone and Matt Orr to the case. They had been doing very well using two minivans, and they were resourceful in the face of obstacles. Early on they discovered that the subject worked for a garbage company and went to work at four a.m. They followed him to work one morning, but the garbage company was surrounded by a high fence that didn't allow them to see inside. As the twenty or so garbage trucks left the property in the darkness every morning, it was impossible to see which one was carrying the subject.

Orr came up with an idea. He didn't shave for a couple of days and showed up at 4:15 a.m. at the garbage company wearing a red bandana on his head. He looked scruffy. Canone waited outside in his minivan while Orr went into the office and applied for a job. All the while he was able to keep the subject in view and watched as the guy threw his lunch bag and thermos into the cab of truck number twenty-eight.

When number twenty-eight came out, the tail started. As the sun rose and photography was possible, the two minivans tag-teamed the garbage truck. The most notable segment of videotape was when the subject leaned over and, without help, wrapped his arms around a clothes dryer and hefted it up and into the back of the garbage truck. He is then shown walking away with no apparent aftereffects. So much for that bad back.

Ward became our cheerleader at State Farm and sent many more cases our way. State Farm also tasked us with setting up a special project in which we supplied them with three full-time employees to work out of the Runnemede, New Jersey, claim office. Their duties were to take photos of accident scenes and vehicle damage and pick up police reports. This worked well for both State Farm and us. The inside claims representatives were able to keep their files up to date, and we had a steady, ongoing project. This arrangement worked for three years before someone at State Farm came up with an alternative plan.

CHAPTER SEVENTEEN

The New Jersey Insurance/Legal System:
"Friggin' in the Riggin'"

Let's face it: insurance companies are in business to make money. To make a profit, their premium intake has to exceed the total of their claim losses and administrative expenses. Insurance companies are closely regulated by their state's insurance commission, so they cannot boost their premiums whenever they want. They must take their case to the state and argue for any adjustments. Traditionally, this was a slam dunk for the insurance carriers. All they had to do was submit the numbers to show how badly they were doing, and they always got their way.

Then everything changed. Politicians entered the fray, and the New Jersey legislature began to insist that insurance carriers fight insurance fraud more aggressively. Special investigation units (SIUs) were mandated. To comply, the companies hired ex-cops with some insurance acumen to go after fraud and then settled back, figuring that would satisfy the state.

After a while the state recognized that nothing much had improved. Interviews with SIU directors made it clear that the regular claims departments resented the SIUs trampling on their turf. Cases that should have been transferred to the SIU were kept and handled, albeit poorly from a fraud investigation perspective, by the regular claims staff. The SIU was relegated to window dressing to satisfy rate increases. Again, the state came down on the carriers, insisting that they really fight fraud.

The higher-ups at Allstate, my alma mater, hit the ceiling. Allstate said it was withdrawing from New Jersey and went so far as transferring employees to other states, closing down some offices, and otherwise acting like they really meant to take their marbles and scram. The state eventually caved and Allstate is still in New Jersey and doing just fine. A decade later, State Farm played the same game and got its way, as well.

Fraud is a serious public issue. In a perfect world the injured party would submit an honest and unembellished claim to the insurance company, which would pay it accordingly. Unfortunately, that is not always the case, so we have a civil system in which a plaintiff brings his or her claim forward, making allegations that the insurance company has every right to verify.

Enter the plaintiff's attorney, whose fee is based on the amount recovered. Usually, the plaintiff's attorney ends up with a third of the settlement or judgment up to $100,000 and maybe 10 percent of the amount above that figure. It varies from state to state, and other conditions apply as well. So, the more serious the case can be portrayed, the higher the recovery and, of course, the more money the plaintiff's attorney takes home. Some call it embellishment. I call it fraud.

The insurance companies aren't blameless, either. When I worked at Allstate, a lawsuit would be filed and the first thought would be to see who the plaintiff's lawyer was. Some law firms were referred to as "pioneers," meaning they were considered "early settlers," thus earning no respect from the claims staff. They were pushovers and not worthy of concern. The really tough plaintiff's law firms wouldn't even talk to a claims adjuster and waited until the courthouse steps to enter into negotiations. So, if an injured party had a legitimate claim but was represented by an attorney who was not from one of the aggressive and well-known plaintiff's law firms, that claim got no respect, the attorney would be pushed around, and the injured party's recovery would suffer.

If the injured party hired the right firm, however, the case would be transferred up the chain and the dance would begin. The plaintiff's attorney would build up the case, often stepping over the line in doing so. Again, this had much less to do with righting a wrong and much more to do with how far both sides could push each other. The system is rife with opportunity for fraud.

One might ask: If a fraudulent or overstated claim is discovered, why aren't criminal charges filed? Isn't fraud a crime? Our agency investigated literally thousands of civil cases during our decades working for insurance companies in New Jersey, New York, Pennsylvania, and Florida. Even when we had videotape proof that a claimant was physically able to perform certain activity in direct conflict with his or her allegations (which was often), pushing a criminal fraud case never seemed to be a major consideration. After all, it has always been about the money, not what is right or wrong. The plaintiff's bar continues to get away with stretching the truth, and the insurance companies continue in their role of asking the state's permission to pass the losses on to the good drivers, who pay more and more in premiums every year.

Occasionally, an insurance company special investigation unit busts an insurance crime ring. Crooked lawyers who send their clients to crooked doctors to inflate cases are sometimes caught and brought to justice, as are people who stage accidents. I recall an incident where the New Jersey Insurance Department, Fraud Division, had a dump truck intentionally rear-end an empty bus in downtown Jersey City, New Jersey, during rush hour. Within two weeks "bus passengers," claiming all sorts of injuries, had filed sixty claims. Arrests followed, including some complicit doctors and lawyers.

That was impressive, but it didn't come anywhere near addressing the constant flow of thousands of overstated claims that go under the radar. Until the insurance companies really start going after fraud, premiums will not come down. That applies to medical malpractice, workers' compensation, disability, and all aspects of insurance where fraud is tolerated.

Occasionally, however, someone comes close to hitting back.

Federal Judge Marion Trump Barry: "You Are Lucky I Am Trying the Law and Not the Facts in This Case or I Would Think You Were Trying to Perpetrate a Fraud on My Court."

The following case shows just how far a plaintiff's attorney will go to nudge a jury into a large payday for the plaintiff and, of course, the lawyer, himself. It also demonstrates the effectiveness of solid videotape evidence.

Attorney Joe Burns, who was going to trial on a case we had investigated months before, needed us to put our videotape into evidence in federal court in Trenton. Burns explained that the plaintiff's attorney was going all out to demonstrate the long-term damage done to his client. During the trial that client (let's call her Mrs. A.) was pressing her back against the side wall of the courtroom, grimacing in pain. The investigating police officer, the plaintiff's doctors, and others gave their testimony, and all the time Mrs. A.'s back pain was vividly on display for the jury. The Honorable Marion Trump Barry, the older sister of real estate tycoon Donald Trump, showed sympathy for Mrs. A. and allowed her the wall space at counsel's request.

When our time came to testify, Burns called me to the stand. I was sworn in and in response to his questions explained that we had videotape evidence to introduce.

As soon as I spoke those words, the plaintiff's attorney leapt to his feet, exclaiming, "Surprise! Your honor, I claim surprise. I was not made aware in discovery of this videotape and strenuously object to the introduction of this evidence." Mrs. A., the wallflower, continued to act out her painful existence, her face pitifully scrunched up in brave forbearance.

Judge Barry turned to Burns with a frown. "Well, Mr. Burns, what do you say to that?" Barry ruled her courtroom firmly and did not put up with lawyer grandstanding from either side.

Burns got up and said with great deference to the judge, "Your honor, under federal rules I do not have to reveal anything to opposing counsel if he does not specifically ask for it. In this case, counsel failed to ask the question, so I am not compelled to give it up prior to trial." He went on to provide the proper citation from the federal rule book.

The tapping of the judge's pen could be heard over the sound system as she reflected on Burns's argument, then made her decision. The jury was sent out in order for the court to review the video evidence first. She leaned forward in her chair and cautioned, "I have seen so many of these videotapes where you can't even identify the subjects. After five days of testimony, Mr. Burns, I am not going to allow this jury to be subjected to inferior evidence just so you can try to score points. I will not tolerate any nonsense."

As Mrs. A. continued holding up the side wall, the lights went out and the television screen lit up. Judge Barry slid her chair to one side so she could see the television, but not without an impatient glance in Burns's direction that said, "This better be good!"

A clear shot of Mrs. A. filled the screen. She was on her apartment balcony banging on the gutter above her head with the handle of a broom, trying to break up the ice clinging there. This required her to bend over backward and reach out in an awkward position. She also had some laundry on the balcony to dry and could be clearly seen bending over for several minutes at a time rearranging the laundry on the portable clothes rack. She then stood upright without any apparent restriction or indication that she was in pain. Her actions on the videotape totally belied her in-court antics.

We also followed Mrs. A. as she went on shopping trips. Again, Linda's videotape showed her pushing the shopping cart with a normal gait. There was no limping or any other suggestion of pain or physical difficulty. The videotape left no doubt in anyone's mind that Mrs. A. was overacting in court that day.

When the lights came back on in the courtroom, the plaintiff's lawyer was on his feet about to continue his objections when Judge Barry leaned forward, eyes blazing. Cutting him off, she said, "You sit down! After five days of testimony and watching your client's antics in my courtroom, you'd better believe this jury is going to see this videotape. You are lucky I am trying the law and not the facts in this case, Mr. Papier, or I would think you were trying to perpetrate a fraud on my court."

What she meant by that last comment was that there was a jury deciding the facts of the case and she was there to act on legal questions that would arise.

The jury returned to view the videotape evidence. I watched the reaction of some of the jurors, who looked away from the screen to Mrs. A. holding up the wall. They had a whole new perspective and came back with a verdict for the defense. Mrs. A. left the courthouse no richer than when she arrived. Her attorney left with his tail between his legs, having been chewed out by a very unamused federal judge.

This case demonstrates how important quality videography can be in a trial. All the legal wrangling and witness testimony aside, nothing matches the sight of a person doing all the things they have sworn in depositions and trial that they cannot do. Video evidence is devastating to the plaintiff and extremely difficult to overcome. Let's do a couple more.

Workers' Compensation Petitioner's Attorney: "My Immigrant Client Does Not Speak English, and Her Injury Precludes Finding Gainful Work."

In the New Jersey workers' compensation system, as in most states, the petitioner (the injured employee) does not have to prove liability but is still entitled to monetary compensation. Workers cannot sue their bosses directly, so the remedy available at law is workers' compensation.

In New Jersey there is a quirky section of the law known as "odd lot." When an injury is such that one cannot work *and* the employee does not speak the language or is encumbered in some other way, the petitioner's lawyer will move to place the matter into the odd lot category. This makes the employee eligible for a greater payout, tantamount to being paid for permanent total disability. Of course, the lawyer also fares better.

In this case, the insurance company doubted the validity of the odd lot claim and asked us to take a closer look at the petitioner. Mrs. Lee was a Korean national in the United States on a work visa. She worked in a noodle factory and had her middle three fingers tragically severed in a noodle machine down to, but not including, the first knuckle. No doubt, she suffered a serious injury and was entitled to workers' compensation. The issue here, however, was whether or not she qualified for odd lot status.

Our investigator followed Mrs. Lee to an indoor flea market on US 1 in New Brunswick one morning. Once inside, he found her at a booth selling fake fur coats. He lingered nearby for a few moments and overheard her speaking in English to a customer.

Linda and I visited Mrs. Lee in her booth. It was the Christmas season, so I concealed our then-bulky Panasonic camcorder in a brightly wrapped box with a flip lid that allowed the lens to peek out. Linda posed as a customer. Mrs. Lee greeted us pleasantly and helped Linda try on several fur jackets while I had the Panasonic whirring away.

Her English, while thickly accented, was quite passable. Not only that, she had a homemade prosthetic device over the stubs of her lost three fingers and deftly connected and worked the zippers of the jackets for Linda.

She was not only gainfully employed and spoke understandable English, but she also had successfully overcome her disability with an innovative homemade prosthetic device. I certainly gave her credit for all those things, but she did not qualify for odd lot. Her attorney got caught pushing the system too far.

Unlike liability cases, in workers' compensation there is no discovery, so opposing counsel was not forewarned of our video and audio evidence. (It is legal to record voice conversations in New Jersey as long as one of the parties is aware of being recorded. Not all states allow that.) We went to the hearing and played our videotape for the judge.

It is well recognized by lawyers that workers' compensation court is heavily weighted in favor of the petitioner/employee. Insurance companies don't do well in comp. court unless they can produce overwhelming evidence that no judge can ignore. In this case, our evidence resulted in Mrs. Lee's odd lot status being removed, and she received the workers' compensation she should have been eligible for in the first place. Again, quality videography surpassed all other evidence and justice was achieved.

Here's another one.

"Uh-oh. She Knows We Are Watching Her. What Now?"

I am often asked, "Do people ever catch you watching them?" While we try to avoid that by using nondescript vans and blending into our surroundings, it does happen from time to time. But it doesn't necessarily mean we quit and go home.

One spring afternoon, Joe Canone called in from a surveillance and said, "We were doing great following her, then she looked straight at me and we locked eyes. She knew. What do we do now?"

The crew had been conducting a two-van surveillance on a female claimant who was asserting neck and back pain and an inability to walk any distance. They explained they had some good videotape of her walking normally across a parking lot with a friend and a child. They had followed her to a liquor store, and just before she went in, she stared hard at one of the minivans. The crew was sure she spotted the surveillance.

Given that we had good videotape of her moving in a normal manner, I thought we should hang in there and see what else she did. I sent the other investigator (the one she didn't spot) into the liquor store to buy a six-pack. He saw her talking animatedly on the phone, probably with her lawyer. I instructed the team to stay in place and see what she did next.

She left after a half hour, and that's when the case turned entirely in our favor. When she came out, she was staring directly at the van with a concerned look on her face. Now, however, she walked with a demonstrable limp that had just developed since the phone call in the liquor store.

Our report included the fact that we believed the plaintiff picked up on our surveillance causing her change in demeanor. She could have just walked out normally and argued that she was having a good day, and that on other days she was in great pain. Instead, her actions demonstrated her intent to commit fraud upon the insurance company. Ultimately, that case settled for the insurance company's offer.

Insurance surveillance work boils down to being in the right place at the right time. It requires patience, the right equipment, and boldness when needed. We never did anything to set up a plaintiff, such as flattening tires or some other action to entrap them. We let them undo their own cases by documenting them in activity that was contrary to their claim allegations.

The best scenario is to end up with comparisons— that is, two separate video segments that portray behavior (1) when the plaintiff knows he or she is being scrutinized and (2) when he or she thinks no one is watching.

There is one other scenario we look for. When an injury claim is initiated, the defendant insurance company has the legal right to have the plaintiff examined by an independent doctor. There are physicians who conduct these physical exams on a regular basis for insurance companies and testify as expert witnesses.

We get involved by setting up our surveillance van in the parking lot or on a nearby street and film the plaintiff going in and out of the doctor's office. Invariably, the limp or other manifestation of physical limitation is on display for the doctor and his staff.

A couple of weeks later, when the plaintiff is going about his or her normal routine, we conduct surveillance to see if the plaintiff's behavior is at odds with the videotape on the day of the physical exam. Again, this can be devastating to the plaintiff's case and shows a conscious intent to defraud and overstate the claim.

We have even had cases where the plaintiff acted out pitiable behavior at the examining physician's office, then would stop at a mall on the way home and exhibit none of those physical limitations on display at the doctor's office just moments before.

Linda's quote to an unhappy plaintiff's lawyer while riding down in the courthouse elevator described it best: "I guess you should have kept her in a body cast, right?"

In most of our cases involving surveillance, we were able to obtain videotape evidence of the subject without his or her knowledge. We just tried to capture the plaintiff acting normally—getting into and out of a car without any demonstrable difficulty, walking up and down the grocery aisles and reaching the upper shelves without the slightest grimace, walking the dog around the block with a normal gait. In all cases, it simply portrayed real life—not the claim file's impression or the other side's allegations.

There were also those cases where we were able to

document the plaintiff's injuries. That is, when we saw someone limping or exhibiting physical difficulty that did, indeed, relate to his or her claim allegations, we photographed that, as well. In those cases it was a benefit to the insurance company to know this claim was not phony. The company could then rethink its defensive stance and enter into meaningful negotiations with the other side and settle the case without the expense of trial.

There is one odd thing about doing surveillance work for insurance companies that deserves a remark. The trial lawyers hired by the insurance companies to defend these lawsuits know that their track record of wins and losses, as well as the quality of their negotiations and settlements, dictate their future assignments from that company. When we submit good surveillance evidence, defense counsel is often put on the spot because they then have no excuse for losing the case.

POLKA, ANYONE?

Early in our private investigation career, we were assigned a surveillance case by Hercules Powder Company in South River, New Jersey. One of its employees was out of work claiming a back injury, and the company thought he was overstating his workers' compensation claim.

Linda and I tried several times to follow the fellow, but the neighborhood was packed with small houses set close together, offering nowhere to park our van without attracting attention. Finally, in frustration I told Linda one

Saturday morning, "I'm gonna give this one more shot. Maybe the streets will be more crowded on a weekend."

I went to South River in our old blue Dodge van and took a pass by the subject's house. Lo and behold, the guy was out in the driveway cleaning his car. I parked right across the street from his house and got out wearing my hard hat and carrying a clipboard. He smiled. I smiled. No problem. I walked around taking numbers off telephone poles, then got back in the van and started videotaping.

The man decided the trunk of his car needed special attention. He actually climbed into the trunk and energetically swept it out. Some of the positions he got into would have qualified him for Cirque du Soleil. His actions thoroughly refuted his claim.

A couple of weeks after I turned in my report and videotape, the client from Hercules called me, hardly able to contain himself. He said, "When the union rep came in to discuss the case with me, I showed him the videotape and your stills, Dave. All he wanted to know is if we caught him at the polka contest, too!"

Chapter Eighteen

It's Not All about Surveillance

I fear I may be giving the impression that all private investigators do is surveillance work. Not so. Taking statements and searching records are also important investigative tools. In fact, not much gets done without doing an initial record check before undertaking any kind of inquiry.

The more we know about someone we intend to deal with, the better. We need to know if anyone associated with a particular case has a criminal record. Do we need to approach this carefully or maybe not take on this case at all? Sometimes we just want to know the person's socio-economic situation before beginning any investigative activities. Does he or she live in a trailer or a castle? Is there anything in his or her record that would be important to know before knocking on the door? Where does this person work, and what does he or she do for a living? All of this information goes into doing proper research ahead of time and lets us know what to expect when we deal on a person-to-person level.

Taking statements is an art. Lawyers on both sides of a legal matter often want potential witnesses interviewed and statements taken—often, but not always.

In Pennsylvania discovery is total. Both sides are entitled to every scrap of paper the opposition has found during an investigation. Pennsylvania lawyers, therefore, usually prefer a phone call before we put a report on paper. Statements, however, are fair game just about everywhere and must be disclosed. Again, the astute Pennsylvania lawyer will want a written statement from the witness with information that helps our case, but not from the witness who harms our case. That may not seem fair to the layperson, but it is based on the premise that both sides are represented and we shouldn't have to do the other side's work for them.

In other areas, however, most attorneys want statements no matter where the facts come down. That also holds true for insurance claims departments. Here's a case where a statement turned the case upside down.

"DOPEY BROAD, SHE SHOULDA WORN FLATS."

This one started off as a surveillance case. The subject (let's call her Gloria) alleged a serious injury to her right knee caused by a motor vehicle accident. Gloria was driving her boyfriend's brand new Audi A5, and while she was stopped at a traffic light, the insured's truck hit her in the rear. This was a case of full liability against the driver of the truck with a policy issued by our insurance company client. They knew they would have to make a payout, but just how much was the question.

According to an expert hired by the insurance company, Gloria's knee injury was not consistent with having occurred during an auto accident. Further, her constant complaints seemed to be a bit overstated given the specific nature of her injury. But that testimony would not be enough on its own, so surveillance of the plaintiff was deemed appropriate.

Gloria worked in an office in Newark. She parked her car in the same spot each day but varied her route out of the area when she left. Our crew reported that she was very cagey behind the wheel, always looking around. Worse, her office desk was next to a large window, giving her full view of the parking lot, which was the only place we could set up to see her car when she left.

I reported back to the insurance company's lawyer that this was not a case where surveillance work would likely bring positive results. I asked the attorney for more facts to see if there was some other way to approach this. She faxed over the accident report and I saw that the Audi belonged to a male about Gloria's age. The attorney said the insured owner of the Audi, believed to be Gloria's boyfriend, had not been found. I said I would give it a try and see what he had to say. The accident had happened more than two years prior, so it was possible they were no longer together.

The boyfriend (let's call him Freddie) was no longer at the address provided in the accident report and no one there knew where he moved. All efforts to come up with an address for Freddie failed until I contacted his mother. She said that Freddie had moved in with her when he lost his job and that he would be home after seven p.m. that night.

Freddie was a little suspicious at first. He asked, "Who are you working for?"

"The insurance company hired me to investigate this accident. I am not working for Gloria. Can you help me out here?"

"That bitch! She didn't hurt her knee in that accident. She fell on the stairs leading to my mother's back deck. She had those stupid six-inch spike heels on. Her heel got caught in the space between the boards and she went straight down on her knee. Then, when the accident happened two weeks later, she thought she could get away with claiming that's how she got hurt. Dopey broad, she shoulda worn flats."

I took a detailed statement from Freddie, which delighted our attorney client, as well as the insurance company. Gloria, however, would have none of this. She adamantly denied Freddie's version of the accident on the stairs and held firm to her story.

We then obtained hospital records that showed Gloria's knee injury took place two weeks before the motor vehicle accident. The lawsuit was dismissed, and our job was finished.

Statements can be powerful. They seldom get into evidence in court, however, because of something known as the "best evidence rule." That is, actual testimony of the witness is required, not just the statement. There are exceptions. A statement might be admissible to refute changed testimony. Remember Mr. Brown and " . . . then the roof fell in?" That statement got into evidence only because Mr. Brown said, " I . . . can't . . . talk." The statement impeached his prior testimony, thus was admissible.

Also, a dying declaratory statement may be entered directly into evidence when the witness is no longer available.

Basically, a statement is a commitment to testify if called upon. Both sides of a lawsuit seek to show the opposition the strength of their case, and the statement plays a major role in that effort. One of the principal rules of taking a statement is to make it brief and to the point. Later on in the proceedings, the lawyers will hold depositions where a great deal of detail is covered. The statement is the gateway to getting facts moving in that direction.

"It Wasn't Me. . . . I Didn't Hit Anybody!"

A private investigator engaged by a law firm brings more to the table than a photographer or a record searcher. All the investigator's contacts and expertise are there for the lawyer to best serve the client. There are times, however, when the unexpected occurs.

There was a foot of snow on the ground and the roads were still being plowed. It got dark before five p.m.

in New Jersey this time of year, so visibility wasn't that great, but traffic along US 202 south of Somerville was moving along well enough for our client. He was driving an eighteen-wheeler for a local milk bottling company and had left the plant about a half hour before. John (not his real name) was a family man with twelve years of professional driving experience.

As John motored along a little below the posted speed limit, he sipped coffee from his thermos and occasionally responded to other truckers on his CB radio. The CB repartee helped overcome the boredom that came with the job. Naturally, guiding his tractor-trailer down the road under these conditions meant he had to keep a sharp watch on the four-wheelers around him, because, as we all know, eighteen-wheelers don't stop on a dime.

At that same moment, Mary (also not her real name) was on the way back home from doing some grocery shopping and was driving in the opposite direction from John. Mary was shocked to see a dark figure at the side of the road suddenly step right out in front of that northbound tractor trailer. Even though dressed in dark clothes, the person was illuminated by the truck's headlights for just a second and then vanished. Mary had no doubt that the truck hit the person. She slowed and looked back over her shoulder to see that the big rig didn't even slow down. It just kept going northbound.

Mary called 911 to report the accident, but was too shook up to stop. She was able, however, to report to the police dispatcher the name of the milk company in big letters on the side of the trailer.

Another witness to the same accident was shoveling his driveway for the second time that day, cursing the snowplows for filling his entrance back in. This time Stanley (not his real name) stopped shoveling and looked up at the oncoming headlights, unable to discern whether it was the dreaded plow or not. He could see those headlights and hear the roar of the engine, but it took a few seconds to rule out the plow. It was just another tractor-trailer motoring along the highway. He was just about to go back to his shoveling when his eye caught a man dressed in dark clothes leap out in front of the oncoming truck.

Stan heard the thud just steps away from his driveway entrance and saw the man being propelled forward, then disappear under the truck. Stan remained frozen in place for a moment. Then he tentatively stepped out onto the roadway, and with his snow shovel raised he flagged down the next car before the person lying still on the roadway could be hit again.

Three days later, Flemington Attorney Lee Roth called me to his office. He explained that the Hunterdon County Prosecutor's Office was investigating his client, the milk bottling company, concerning a highway death. Witnesses had identified the company's logo on the side of the trailer as it went by.

John was identified as the only driver who could have been in that area at that time on that day. He denied he was involved in this accident. He was adamant. "It wasn't me. I didn't hit anybody. I don't know what they are talking about!"

Roth and I sat down with John in the lawyer's conference room and slowly interviewed him. We took him through his entire trip. John would not budge, and he was very convincing. He said there was no way he could have hit anyone, and if he had, he would say so. "It's a case of mistaken identity."

John was composed and seemingly natural in his response; yet there was something about his body language that troubled me. Then there were those witnesses. How could they not know that milk company logo that goes up and down this part of US 202 all the time? I said, "John, we believe you, but these witnesses seem certain that it was one of your company trucks involved. Tell you what, I know a way of clearing this up."

I gave a quick glance over at Roth. He nodded and I went on. "John, if you will let me bring in a guy who will ask you some questions on tape it might help. He will then run the tape against a machine that measures stress and such. It's a fairly new science, and I think it will help clear you if you are telling us the truth."

Lou Greer, a fellow former Plainfield Police detective, was now offering psychological stress evaluator (PSE) testing. If John were telling us the truth, we would know which way to go with our investigation. If not, then John could be put on the spot, and we could work on his defense from that perspective.

Greer showed up on time and, as always, chewing on his unlit cigar. He set up the PSE in Roth's office and John submitted to the testing. The graph spewed from the machine for about ten minutes; then came the post-exam analysis.

"John, here is where I asked you if you knew anything about the accident," Greer explained. "See how the graph reacted? Here is where I asked you if you were telling me the whole truth. Again, see how it reacted?" Greer was good at this.

Suddenly John's face reddened. Tears welled up and a gasping sound came from his throat. He blurted out, "I am so sorry. I couldn't believe anyone would jump out in front of me. I didn't mean it. I just froze behind the wheel. Then after it happened it was so dark and snowy, I thought I was the only one who saw it, so I just kept going. I knew he had to be dead. It's not like I was trying to get away with anything. It was more like I couldn't believe it happened and I had to escape from a bad dream. I am so sorry!" He sobbed for several minutes.

Roth met with the prosecutor, who agreed to pursue no charges other than "leaving the scene of an accident." John agreed to a guilty plea, and the case was resolved.

John apparently suffered from post-traumatic stress immediately following the accident, thus explaining his steadfast denial that the accident even happened. He had convinced himself that it was all a lie, but placing the PSE graph in front of him broke through his psychological block and allowed him to face the truth.

The witness statements of Mary and Stan provided strong evidence that this was a suicide-by-truck case. The manner in which the man leapt in front of the truck and actually faced it in the middle of the lane was good enough for the prosecutor to forego more serious charges. Further, additional inquiry by the prosecutor's staff revealed the decedent was having emotional issues of his own, which only added to the conclusion this was a suicide.

Roth kept that PSE graph and had it enlarged. It is framed and hangs in his office as a reminder that sometimes you have to find a way to deal with your client to reach a happy ending.

HE WASN'T SPEEDING

The receptionist said, "Mr. Broscious will see you now, Mr. Watts." Jim Broscious was a young and aggressive plaintiff's attorney in Warren County, New Jersey. There was a hint of arrogance in his mannerisms, but I figured that was just youth trying to play in the big leagues. As a group, it is fair to say that plaintiff's lawyers tend to be more aggressive than their peers in other aspects of legal practice.

"Come in, Dave, and thanks for coming so quickly. I have just taken on a one-car fatal accident case and I need a full workup. The client is the father of the dead kid and doesn't like the way the police handled their investigation. The cops say the kid was speeding. The client says it can't be."

Jim went on to explain that the client's twenty-four-year-old son was driving his late-model Triumph TR3 when it flipped over, killing him instantly. This happened on a rural country road that had lots of curves and ups and downs. Our first thoughts were that a young man driving alone over challenging roads in a sports car was, indeed, probably going too fast and lost control, but it certainly deserved a closer look.

The father swore his son was not like that. "No, he was a careful driver. His wife just had a baby, and he was a very responsible young man. He had just come into the business with me, too." Frankly, at that point I had my doubts. All kids act up from time to time, right?

I opened a file and began the usual preliminaries. I reviewed the police report and visited the scene. I took photos and measurements and canvassed the area for witnesses. What I really wanted was to inspect the car, but I was informed the insurance company had already disposed of it.

I requested a title search from the New Jersey Department of Motor Vehicles and learned that the title had passed through a salvage yard and then to George Felegy. There was no address for Felegy, so I had to do some more digging before coming up with his address on top of the Kittatinny mountain range in northwestern New Jersey.

When I pulled up to the Felegy farmhouse, I was greeted by the biggest and meanest German shepherd ever born. He put his paws on my driver's window and his snarling, curled-back lips left no doubt about his intentions. I was in his yard, and if I got out of the car, I would be staying for lunch and he would be the only one eating.

Felegy came out to the sound of my horn blowing and shooed Thor away. "He won't bite. He's really very friendly." *Don't they all say that? Maybe you know it, George, but does Thor know it?*

Felegy was friendly and open. He was the quintessential grease monkey. Slightly disheveled, dressed in mechanic's overalls, he was about six feet tall and average weight and in need of a haircut. I showed him my P.I. identification and asked him about the Triumph TR3 he bought at salvage.

"Yeah, I bought it for parts. Got rid of most of it, though. Had no room in the barn for both of them. All I know is it was crushed down at the junk yard."

I was disappointed. Often physical damage on accident vehicles can tell the story better than anything else. "Well, George, I tried. Thanks for your time," I said, and started to get back into the car.

Then Felegy offered, "But I do know what caused that accident."

I was doubtful but listened to his theory. After all, I drove all the way up here and he had been cooperative. What he said next blew my mind.

"Yeah, that little car flipped over because the right rear spring broke just before the curl. Broken spring, for sure." Felegy went on to say that when he took the TR3 apart, he threw that right rear spring and a fender behind the barn. We went back there and found them in the tall grass that had grown up around them. Felegy allowed me to take photos of him and the spring in place, as well as a few close-ups of the spot on the spring where it was broken and, of course, the remaining right front fender.

"Looks to me like some kind of corrosion made it break," Felegy said. "See the flaky metal in the center of the break?"

Oh, man, I thought. *What we have here is a product liability case against an automaker, and the chain of evidence is preserved. Wait till Broscious sees this!*

I took a statement from Felegy while Thor sat eyeing my left leg. Felegy enjoyed the attention and eventually made an excellent witness in the case. The car was gone, but the critical evidence had stayed, waiting for months in the weeds behind a barn out in the wilderness of the Kittatinny Mountains. After both Felegy and I signed a dated receipt for the spring, I toted it back to Broscious's office.

Because British Leyland was the manufacturer of the TR3, this auto accident case became international in nature. As defendants go, carmakers are tough opponents, and British Leyland was no exception. The company immediately denied any liability.

Broscious knew he had a fight on his hands. He would have to employ expert witnesses to prove the corrosion theory, so he and I took a couple of trips. First we met with an expert metallurgist in Detroit, where we learned the spring had suffered from "fretting corrosion." Further, the expert's examination of the spring brought him to the conclusion that it was made from inferior metal. "Probably from Japan. They save money using this crappy steel."

Next, we flew the fender to Atlanta, where we met with two accident-reconstruction experts. Broscious brought out photos of the accident scene, as well as photos of the car taken by the investigating officers. There was a lot of bantering back and forth, and I stood on the sideline taking it all in. Something in the photos caught my eye.

"Look at the windshield and its frame," I said, thinking out loud. "It seems reasonable that if this convertible were going fast and went all the way over, the windshield and frame would be smashed backwards toward the passenger compartment. Here we can see that it is simply flattened in place. That looks like a slow flip, not the result of a high-speed rollover. I think when he drove over the top of this small hill," I said, pointing back at the scene pictures, "the spring broke, causing an imbalance, and over she went."

The group of experts went into pause mode, blinked, and looked at each other. Slowly they nodded their heads. There are times when just plain common sense is part of an analysis. Experts sometimes complicate things so they can put their vast knowledge on display.

Broscious was able to get British Leyland to settle the case, even flying on the Concorde to London for a deposition. The system worked, albeit after a long struggle. The wife and family of the young man who lost his life were compensated by the automaker, and British Leyland recalled the TR3s and upgraded the rear springs. Broscious, meanwhile, had the actual spring bronzed, and it hung in his office over his desk until he died.

"A Lion Mauled Me . . ."

John Coley was an attorney in the Kunzman, Coley, Yospin law firm in Watchung, New Jersey. (The Kunzman in the firm is the same Judge Kunzman who signed our search warrants back in the Plainfield Special Squad.) Coley called me to say he was trying to settle an estate but could not find any relatives of the decedent, Elvida Petrella, a longtime resident and spinster in the Watchung area. She had no will, and no one seemed to have any knowledge of her family history. Coley had taken it as far as he could and needed some investigative help.

"If I can't come up with a qualified relative, the assets of Elvida's estate will escheat to the State of New Jersey, David," Coley explained. "There's a lot of money and real estate involved. She never married and had no children that we know of. I need you to find a living family member."

This was a record-searching case. Linda and I had lots of experience searching old records—not particularly glamorous, but challenging, nevertheless.

First we did the obvious by talking to her neighbors

and other contacts. Nothing. Then we went to the Somerset County Clerk's office and pulled old deeds, mortgages, judgments, and the like. Again, nothing.

Finally, we asked one of the county employees where they kept the old miscellaneous records—that is, files and correspondence that didn't fall into a particular category, yet were kept in storage by the county. We were directed to a section in a dusty basement with rows and rows of small green boxes, some dating back into the 1800s. At first, there didn't seem to be any system to follow in order to find what we were looking for. Then it looked as if the papers were filed by date by section and within each section in alphabetical order.

We began checking each section for all the P files for Petrella. Finally, we came upon a letter written by a Martino Petrella to his nephew in New York City. The envelope was intact and postmarked "Kenya, Sept. 14, 1906." The letter's content was amazing. Martino Petrella wrote that he was working for a surveyor in Africa and had only a couple of months left on his contract. He continued, "I am dying. I was mauled by a lion and am infected now. I sent a porter for help, but I don't think he will get back with help in time for me and I won't see you again."

Now we had a starting point for our investigation. We found that the nephew in New York had died, leaving several offspring, so we contacted one of them. She said without any coaching from us, "Oh, yeah, Grandpa Petrella told us about a cousin Elvida who lived alone out in the country in Jersey. What's this all about?"

Coley was able to take it from there and qualify Elvida's somewhat distant, yet verifiable, family members, who inherited a tidy sum of money and real estate. The letter from a dying man describing his terrible ordeal following the lion attack, and the human emotion conveyed in that letter, was particularly striking to us. Not only did it provide the clue we needed to move the case forward, but it was also a true historic treasure.

Chapter Nineteen

The Sexy Black Widow

She called the receptionist early in the day requesting an after-hours appointment with Dr. R. (real name withheld), a fibromyalgia specialist. She explained she was in pain but could not get to the office before five p.m. She arrived just as the office staff was leaving. She was a blonde in her early forties with clear, pale skin. She looked as if she worked out regularly to keep in shape. Dr. R. met with her in an examination room, and in the hour that followed they engaged in sexual intercourse.

A little background. First, her last husband died of a heart attack on the steps of the courthouse the previous year, leaving her with a nice financial package. Second, she filed a complaint of sexual assault against the Dr. R., claiming he hypnotized and drugged her. Third, she never went to the hospital for an initial examination including a rape kit; instead, she went to her primary-care doctor to report the incident and to be drug tested. Fourth, she then went to the Phoenix Center for the victims of abuse. Last, and perhaps most significantly, she is a licensed practical nurse and surely knows the proper protocol in sexual abuse cases but didn't follow it.

About a week later, Dr. R. and his wife sat in the waiting area of the Wilbur Smith law firm in Fort Myers. I came in at about the same time and sat down nearby and grabbed a magazine. Wilbur had called me earlier in the day to ask me to sit in on his first meeting with the doctor. A distinguished-looking middle-aged man with a full head of graying hair, Dr. R. sat fidgeting uncomfortably while his wife sat staring stoically at the opposite wall. Mrs. R. was short, a bit chubby, and had closely cut dark hair. Later, in the conference room, Dr. R. told his side of the story.

"This patient came in after work and I met with her in one of the exam rooms. It was a bit unusual to extend office hours, but I was told she was in pain, so I tried to accommodate her. Then she came on to me, and I am sorry to say I went along with it. I've never done anything like this before, and I can't believe I fell for it. Foolishly, a couple of days later I called her at home, and she invited me over. After a few minutes of us making small talk, two police detectives stepped out from behind a curtain and arrested me." With his head down, the doctor ended with, "I just want to make this clear: I did not drug that woman, and what we did was not rape!"

While her husband spoke, Mrs. R. sat passively, looking down at her folded hands. When he finished, raising her head slowly, she said quietly yet forcefully, "Mr. Smith, I know my husband. He did a stupid thing and we are working it out; but I know he did not rape that woman. He could not and would not do that." They were both very convincing.

Then more details came out. The "patient" was wearing sexy thong underwear and no bra. It seemed clear to all in the meeting that there was something more behind this incident, requiring an in-depth investigation.

After the couple left, the attorney gave me my marching orders. I was to conduct a background investigation on the woman and report back. Smith made clear my parameters: "There is one catch, however, Dave. It is called the rape shield law. What this means is criminal defense lawyers cannot go after the complainant's past sexual history in rape cases. We have to be careful not to cross that threshold. It's okay to do normal due diligence, but don't do any interviews that might look like we were violating rape shield."

I jumped into this case, and over the next several weeks, the real story came out. I learned that this female patient not only lost her husband recently, but also had been married four times before.

One of the former husbands, Mr. Teelucksing, eloped with her after she dumped her second husband and got a handsome alimony settlement. Mr. Teelucksing also left a wife behind when he eloped with the complainant. I found the former Mrs. Teelucksing in New York City and spoke with her on the phone.

"I knew he was shacking up with her," she said. "They had a nice apartment across the street from where

· Accidental P.I. ·

he and I were supposed to be living as man and wife. Once she wanted to collect welfare, so she asked to use my apartment address so that the social worker would see that she was in dire need for benefits. My place was a dump. My husband, rest his soul now, was not a perfect man, but I loved him just the same. He was a black man, of course, but he had this thing for blondes."

Then I found the woman's most recent boyfriend, a pesticide company employee in south Fort Myers. He didn't want to get involved in the case. "There is no way I want to have anything to do with that woman again," he said. "She is a black widow. She destroys everything and everyone she comes into contact with. Count me out!"

But I kept after him, and one day I caught up with him in the rear parking lot of his workplace, where he opened up to me. "One night we were drinkin' and she asks me if I knew of any rich doctors she could set up to sue. She was runnin' out of money from her last husband's death and wanted to score big time. I'm tellin' you, this broad is bad!"

Meanwhile, Wilbur Smith received a discovery package from the prosecuting attorneys. In that package was a recording of the complainant's interview with the detectives just before they set up the scenario to arrest Dr. R. at her home. A number of us who were working on the case sat around the conference table at the law firm listening to the tape:

"Now, what we want you to do is act normally. We don't want you to say or do anything that could be construed as entrapment. Leave it up to him to bring up anything sexual, especially what happened to you in his office, all right?" The detectives were coaching the witness, but nothing out of the ordinary.

"Suppose I suggest we go into the bedroom. Wouldn't that encourage him?"

"No. Don't do that."

"Maybe I should be wearing something a little more revealing. Waddaya think?"

"No, you are fine the way you are. Just let him put nails in his own coffin."

We could hear the frustration in the detectives' responses. Back in the conference room, all eyes were rolling. One of the paralegals said, "Wow, she is really after this guy!"

Also in that package was a detailed statement by the complainant: "I went to him for treatment for my chronic pain. He asked me the normal questions about my medical history and also my personal life. I told him my husband died about a year ago and I just broke up with my boyfriend. He prescribed some medication, then recommended I undergo pain transference. That involved hypnosis. I told him I didn't think I could be hypnotized, but I let him try anyway. He had me lie down on the examination table and began speaking softly to me. He touched my face and neck, and I could feel heat as the pain began to leave my body. He then began rubbing other parts of my body, including my vaginal area. I was aware of what was happening, but could not open my eyes or move. He began kissing me and putting his hands in my mouth. Then he took off my clothes and helped me to the floor. That's when he raped me. I couldn't open my eyes. I couldn't resist. He gradually released me from the hypnosis and said that he'd like to do it again, just not in his office."

Smith asked me to sit in on his subsequent deposition of the complainant. At one point, he asked her, "And how many times have you been married?"

"I don't know. Maybe three or four."

"Do you remember the first?"

"Yes." She gave the first husband's name.

"How about the second?"

She hesitated and seemed to be giving it some thought. When Smith said the husband's name she said, "Well, I don't consider that one a real marriage."

"How about Teelucksing?"

At that she reared back and said, "Oh my God. You know about him, too?"

The two female prosecutors, who had been relentless in pushing this case forward, shot quick glances at each other. It was apparent they didn't know everything about their star witness.

The case went on for months with both legal teams sparring their way through the process. Along the way, the Florida Board of Medicine received Dr. R.'s voluntary surrender of his physician's license to practice medicine in the State of Florida, as did Arizona, where he also had a license to practice.

The criminal charges shook out as follows: The most serious charge was "lewd and lascivious behavior against an elderly or disabled person." The rationale for this charge was the allegation that the complainant had been drugged, therefore "disabled," when the sexual assault took place, but since that could not be proven, the charge was dropped by the prosecutor. Dr. R. pleaded guilty to aggravated battery and two counts of battery, which earned him a ten-year prison sentence and two concurrent one-year sentences. Fortunately for him, he had the right law firm working for him and he received ten years of probation instead of jail time.

This case turned out as it should have. Dr. R. was caught up in the web of an apparently unscrupulous woman who used men regularly for financial purposes. He used bad judgment, for sure, but not to the level of incarceration. Rightfully, he lost his license to practice medicine.

While there's no way to excuse the doctor's behavior, I believe the extenuating circumstances had a lot to do with the sentencing. The manner in which the complainant conducted herself before and during the legal process, as well as her past history, probably influenced the final outcome, in spite of the rape shield law.

Incidentally, to this day there is no record of the complainant ever filing a civil lawsuit against Dr. R., as her former boyfriend had intimated. When that boyfriend gave his deposition (not voluntarily, I assure you), the two prosecutors discounted his testimony as that of a rejected lover who made up the story once he learned of the case.

When I first talked to him, however, he had no knowledge of the criminal case against the doctor, and when he finally spilled the beans regarding her desire to sue a doctor, his recollection of that conversation was very convincing.

The complainant likely learned that in any civil case she brought against the doctor, the rules of the game would be a lot different from criminal court. Her life would be an open book, and her credibility would be on the line. My digging into her background and locating the boyfriend played its part in helping the doctor's case end up where it should have. Major credit goes to attorney Smith, who pulled all the threads together and was able to work the deal with the prosecutor.

HOMICIDE OR SOMETHING ELSE? (HIDE THE KIDS!)

"Hey Dave, George Murtaugh here. Just thought I'd call and let you know they just found a body near Round Valley Reservoir. Could be the dude you've been looking for."

I thanked George, hung up, dropped what I was doing, and raced over to the road leading through the reservoir area. There, about a mile into the state-held property, was the usual gathering of emergency vehicles parked hodgepodge along the edge of the pavement. It wasn't difficult to locate the focus of attention.

One of the Clinton Township, New Jersey, officers

was setting up the yellow crime-scene tape and recognized me when I walked up. "Dave, this could be your guy. Wanna go up?" He gestured over his right shoulder with a jerk of his head up a slight incline toward a circle of men looking down at the ground. All the locals knew about our missing person case, and this looked like it would be an unhappy ending.

"Sure, thanks." I ducked under the yellow crime scene tape and climbed up to a grassy shelf about twenty-five feet in from the roadway and joined the group. Two prosecutor detectives were there, in subdued discussion with the county medical examiner. They were debating the least damaging method of moving the remains. A couple of firemen stood off to the side, staring at the corpse on the ground.

As I walked up, I saw an adult male posed on his knees and in a leaning forward position. The condition of the body suggested it had been exposed a long time to the weather and animal predation. The skin was leathery and the lower jaw was separated from the head and about six feet away. Teeth were scattered about the area and there were chew marks on the top of the head, revealing parts of the skull underneath. He was fully dressed in casual slacks and a long-sleeved shirt and had what looked like white sneaker laces wound tightly around his neck. He was barefoot, and no shoes were found at the scene.

The detectives and the medical examiner were waiting for a sheet of four by eight-foot plywood to arrive. They intended to transfer the remains onto the plywood for transport, thereby keeping the body intact for additional forensic examination.

The medical examiner commented, "It'll be tough to come up with date of death considering the condition of the body, but it looks like a strangulation cause. Off the cuff, I'd say it's been out here for weeks."

One of the detectives leaned over closer and said, "His hands and fingers are still intact, so we might be able to get a decent set of fingerprints by peeling and rolling."

I told them that the body was the right size and, from what I could discern, seemed to be the right age for the man we had been looking for over the past six weeks. Indeed, fingerprints ultimately confirmed the body was that of Chris (not his real name), our missing man.

Six Weeks Earlier

Attorney Al Rylak called and asked me to meet with him and a client at his office. The initial phone call went like this: "Dave, I have to ask you to be a little forbearing in this case. My client is gay and his live-in partner has disappeared. At this point it is a missing person case, but because of the evidence so far, we fear foul play."

I met with Al and his client, Sam (not his real name), who explained he had come home from a local political meeting to find the house empty, their new bronze-colored Chrysler gone, and a mess in the den. Half-empty beer cans were strewn on the wooden tabletop, something Chris, his neatnik partner, would never do, and a floor lamp was knocked over. There was also a jar of what Sam called "enabling cream" on the side table, leading Sam to believe there had been sexual activity in the den.

Sam explained that Chris didn't answer his cell phone when Sam tried to call him that night. When he went out to the garage area, Sam saw two drag marks in the gravel leading up to where Chris usually parked the Chrysler. Really worried now, Sam called the police. Two troopers from the local state police barracks responded and took down the information.

Sam sat wringing his hands, as he described the beginning of this ordeal. "They were not sympathetic at all. One asked if we had a lover's quarrel, and the other one just snickered the whole time. They poured one can of beer into the other and kept it "as evidence," and threw the empty one in the trash. I was livid, but there was nothing I could do at that point."

Sam said that he then went around to all the local bars looking for Chris and learned that he was last seen at a small bar on Route 173, just off Interstate 78, westbound. Sam's theory was that Chris met someone there and brought him back to the house, but things turned bad and something terrible had happened to Chris. This was three days ago, with no word from the missing partner.

Rylak collected a retainer for my services, and I went back to the office to set up the file. I also went to the local police barracks to see if the troopers would share anything with me. They didn't, but they were okay with me looking for Chris. I told them I would let them know if I found anything of interest. It's always wise to let the authorities know when another investigation is going on the same time as theirs. It's also wise to stay out of their way, if possible, and to let them know you will do just that. In this case, it didn't seem as though the troopers were actively investigating Chris's disappearance, anyway.

The client's initial evidence certainly seemed plausible. Bob Becker, one of our agency's young investigators, and I did the rounds of the local watering holes showing a photo of Chris to everyone who sat or stood still long enough. No one had anything for us.

Then came a break in the case, or so we thought. Rylak called to advise that the Chrysler had been located in a New York City parking garage and was being processed for fingerprints.

I asked one of our associate investigators, Tony Trump, to check out the parking garage. Trump and I go back to the Union County Prosecutor's Office where he worked exclusively undercover on gambling and narcotic cases. He was a rough and tumble guy who spoke fluent Spanish and could handle himself well on the street. He had his own one-man investigating business, and his business card had nothing more than his phone number printed in the center. No name, no address . . . just the phone number.

Trump reported back that he interviewed all the parking-garage attendants who could have been on duty from the time of the disappearance to when the car was found. No one remembered the car or who was driving it when it came into the building. He inquired about the security cameras only to find that they were recorded over after a week. The manager was interested only in catching thieves or vandals on camera.

Trump did, however, locate a copy of the parking ticket, which was stamp-dated just after midnight the same night of Chris's disappearance. The timing was perfect for the car to have been driven to New York City.

Then the case began to fade. Linda thought we should check Spruce Run and Round Valley Reservoir roads, " . . . because if the killer is someone from the city, they would be most familiar with both reservoirs and stick to what they know instead of getting lost on back roads. Besides, who wants to ride around too long with a stiff in the trunk of a car you just stole?" Ultimately, she was proven right.

Rylak called and wanted to put his client on the polygraph. Now that the troopers began to take more interest in the case since the Chrysler was found in New York, they would eventually look at Sam as a person of interest in the disappearance of Chris. I connected Rylak with my old buddy, Bruce Snyder, the polygraphist from Pennsylvania. Snyder ran Sam on the poly and did not find any deception in the answers he got.

Then there was no activity for a month until Chris's body was found at Round Valley Reservoir. It is hard to believe that a strangled body found near the side of a rural road could be anything but murder. Also, there was the scene at the house suggesting sexual activity. The drag marks in the gravel and the missing Chrysler mysteriously turning up in a parking garage in New York surely pointed to criminal activity. But it wasn't murder. Chris likely died as the result of an accident. Here's why.

The medical examiner came back with a cause of death: autoerotic asphyxia. Back in the day, this wasn't discussed in normal circles. In fact, in my law-enforcement experience in the sixties, this cause of death was never even mentioned in training. Also called hypoxyphilia, it is a subcategory of sexual masochism in which enhanced arousal occurs during sexual activity by reducing the oxygen to the brain. This can be done with ligatures (as in this case) or even by placing a plastic bag over one's head. Usually, participants have an escape mechanism of some kind, but that doesn't always work. They know they're engaged in a dangerous practice that can result in death, yet they do it anyway.

Apparently, on that night Chris took someone back to the house, and their sexual experimentation went too far. The other person evidently panicked when he couldn't revive Chris. He took the body from the house, dragged it across the driveway to the Chrysler, then dumped him along the road in the reservoir before driving to New York City. Unless he comes forward voluntarily, whoever was with Chris that night will probably never be identified. Not all cases are solved.

CHAPTER TWENTY

Final Thoughts

*H*e awoke with a serious hangover, checked the time, and
stumbled to the fridge. He chugged down the last of
a week-old milk carton, made a sour face, and navigated
unsteadily to the bathroom. When the phone rang, he cringed
in pain, his head exploding.

"What?" he barked at the caller.

The sexy female voice brought him back from the brink
of nausea. "Please help me. I am being followed, and I think
someone is trying to kill me."

Later that night he regretted picking up that call. He
came around slowly, flat on his back in the alley behind Louie's
Bar. It was like coming out of a bad dream, only the painful
knot on the back of his head belied an innocuous nightmare.
He sat upright and had to grab the ground behind him with
both hands so the alley would stop spinning.

"That broad set me up. I should know better by now."

Well, doesn't that bring back the film-noir days of the
quintessential private detective? It's not surprising that

most people think of private investigators that way. Television and movies always give the P.I. a less-than-virtuous persona and make sure he gets beat up a few times before the final curtain. But he always ends up the hero, even if he falls a little short in the purity department.

Reality is what I have tried to convey in this memoir. No knocks on the head. No buxom blond damsels in distress. No bullets flying or harrowing car chases. Sorry. If that's what you expected, you would have been better off renting a video.

Real private investigators are fact finders. Our work picks up where others reach a dead end. Law firms, companies large and small, and individuals call upon private investigators to come up with answers when their own abilities to find those facts fall short. Just because we don't do all those death-defying antics you see in the movies doesn't mean what we do is not exciting or meaningful.

Contributing to a positive outcome in a civil or criminal trial for our client is what we are all about. Saving a company from financial losses by ferreting out the crooks has value to society. Conducting background checks to assure that the bad guys don't achieve positions where they can do damage is vital to our country's welfare. Catching insurance cheats helps keep premiums down for all of us. The list goes on and on.

Private investigators pride themselves on having the resources to tackle assignments whenever needed. With today's technology at their fingertips, investigators subscribe to special restricted databases shared only with

law enforcement. They join organizations, such as the
National Association of Legal Investigators, the purpose
of which has been to elevate private investigators to
professional status.

The classic image of the private investigator has
been replaced by a professional who specializes in getting
answers to difficult questions, usually in a legal setting. He
or she understands what is and isn't evidence and how it
has to be handled to be admissible in a court of law. The
P.I. knows the legal boundaries and stays within them.

Instead of an office above the local pizza parlor next
to elevated train tracks, today's P.I. rents a nice suite in a
business complex and dresses professionally. Yes, there are
times when we have to get "down and dirty" to accomplish
our goals; but, there again, the P.I. is willing to do what
is necessary to get the job done. It is much less glamorous
and more technical and tedious than you might imagine.

My experience as a private investigator has taken
up most of my adult life, and I wouldn't change a
minute of it. While surely unplanned from the start, as
the title of this book implies, it worked out well for us.
My simple beginning as a police patrolman, then army
private, gradually developed into a full-fledged successful
investigation business, and I have many to thank for that.

WHAT IF?

What if Officer Joe Tufaro had not urged me to apply
to the Plainfield Police Department that January day in

1961? What if I had not asked the prosecutor at that murder scene if he had any job openings? What if I had not turned around in Allstate's reception room and spoken up, and what if the Allstate receptionist had responded differently? What if I hadn't joined the Jaycees and met up with Ray Drake who put me onto title searching? What if Commonwealth Title's Bob Hartlaub had not taken a liking to "Team Watts"? What if attorney Bill Albrecht had not hired us for our first investigation? What if that first State Farm case from Beth Ward hadn't come our way? What if . . . what if? My evolution just seemed to fall into place. No master plan—the accidental P.I.

There are lessons in those "What if?" questions. Recognize opportunities and act on them. Be true to yourself and always try to do the best you can. Never settle for "good enough." Get up. Get going. Walk right through openings that present themselves and go for it.

Police officers often ask me, "How do I get to do what you do?"

My stock answer always seems to put them off. "First, you have to make a few contacts, then sooner or later have the courage to quit here."

Starting a private investigation agency, however, is not easy. Since one of the basic requirements is five years of law enforcement, it follows that most private investigators come from the ranks of law enforcement. But the fledgling P.I. comes up against a triple threat.

First, it is difficult to make the transition from criminal to civil law. "Beyond a reasonable doubt" versus a "preponderance of evidence" is hard to grasp when you have been conditioned to see justice from one set of eyes.

Next, your competition will always have a head start on you, and you need to start finding clients.

Last, and maybe the most difficult, you no longer receive a regular paycheck, and you must become a businessperson. That is, you have to cope with advertising, payroll, scheduling, and, of course, managing your budget. It takes perseverance, hard work, and faith in yourself. There will be depressing moments; the real test is to keep going in spite of obstacles.

Linda and I always made our decisions together and were willing to "step out on the ice." It's not that we were carefree or even that we had dumb luck. We made our choices carefully. Because we recognized opportunity and were willing to take risks, success eventually came our way.

Finally, I leave you with these two wonderful quotes:

William Jennings Bryan, Nebraska congressman and three-time U.S. presidential candidate, said, "Destiny is not a matter of chance, it is a matter of choice; it is not a thing to be waited for, it is a thing to be achieved."

St. John XXIII (canonized April 27, 2014) said, "Consult not your fears, but your hopes and your dreams. Think not about your frustrations, but about your unfulfilled potential. Concern yourself not with what you tried and failed in, but with what is still possible for you to do."

The End

(Well, not quite yet)

(Sorry, have to go now . . . the office phone is ringing.)
 "*Yes, you have the right number. Investigations? Yes, that's what we do. How can I help you? You believe your business partner is cheating you? Uh-huh. Uh-huh. Tomorrow afternoon? Okay, let's meet somewhere private. I'm sure we can help.*"

SPECIAL APPRECIATION

Throughout the book I have noted my thanks to many who either guided me or offered me opportunity to grow and succeed. To this point, however, I have not mentioned those whose encouragement and enthusiasm prodded and nudged me to finally get my story on paper and ultimately published. So, in no particular order, here goes:

Susan Gleason, youngest daughter of Officer John V. Gleason, exchanged emails and telephone calls with me. She helped me get some of my facts straight and provided us with a photograph of her father. She was just two months old when he died. A heart-felt thanks to Susan for her assistance, but also for her forbearance in discussing this difficult subject.

Sincere thanks to my editor, Suzie Holly of MacIntosh Books, Sanibel, Florida. She took on the unenviable job of editing my raw manuscript. Her suggestions were insightful. She smoothed out the rough edges and cleaned up my wordiness and redundancy (see what I mean?). I recommend her to any budding or repeat author. She runs a really neat book store on Sanibel, as well.

Ron Base, successful author of the ongoing Sanibel Detective Series, referred me to Suzie Holly, so I owe him, for sure. Ron, a former newspaper journalist, magazine columnist, and movie critic, gave me hope and sage advice back when the idea was germinating. "Hey, go for it. You have a real story to tell. I have to make mine up!" We had some fun conversations in our separate yet complimenting roles of fictional P.I. creator and real-life P.I. Accomplished and recognized as he is, you might still see him hawking his latest private detective book starring fictional character, Tree Callister, in Bailey's Market on Sanibel.

The annual award for patience beyond the call of duty should go to the folks at Mill City Press and Hillcrest Media for putting up with my clumsy efforts at uploading the various aspects of the book: manuscript, photographs, and add-ons. You know . . . teaching the old dog new tricks.

Our friend and financial advisor, Brian Wurdemann of UBS, left no stone unturned to lend assistance. He even took my unedited manuscript and had it printed into a hardbound book just to encourage me to keep going. Brian's never-ending interest in this project, as well as support for my identity theft presentations, continues to be valued beyond measure. He is a true friend.

Our neighbors in Califon, New Jersey, Clark and Kathy DiBlasio, read several early stage chapters and their encouragement helped me keep going when I had some self-doubt. As former Union County residents, they thought it was time somebody talked frankly about the riot in Plainfield. So I did! Their gallery and frame shop in Califon, New Jersey is a must visit. While in Califon, pop in for a super sandwich at Rambo's Store where Donny Friebergs and his staff served as a story testing ground, too.

Florida lunchtimes at The Sunset Grill on Sanibel, with Manager Dave and wait staff, Scott, Carlos, Lisa, Michelle, John, and Fran, was another of my sounding boards. I thank each of them for putting up with my storytelling. I gauged their reactions to the more humorous anecdotes in the book, as they went about their work keeping customers happy. Carlos Perez and John Hunt also critiqued a couple of chapters. Thanks for your patience, guys and gals, and for those great lunches.

Often last, never least, to my wife of fifty-three years, Linda Watts: Honey, you are the greatest. Thanks so much for enduring those times when my head was rummaging around back in the sixties. Hi, I'm back!

CPSIA information can be obtained
at www.ICGtesting.com
Printed in the USA
FSHW021226171019
63098FS